STUDYING CHILDREN AND TRAINING COUNSELORS IN A COMMUNITY PROGRAM

By PAUL H. BOWMAN, WILLIAM J. DIETERICH, ROBERT F. DeHAAN, HENRY HACKAMACK, ROBERT J. HAVIGHURST, LaVONA A. JOHNSON, ROBERT D. KING, *and* LESTER O. LITLE

The Youth Development Series, Number 2

EDITED BY

ROBERT J. HAVIGHURST

THE COMMITTEE ON HUMAN DEVELOPMENT
THE UNIVERSITY OF CHICAGO

P9-APO-366

THE UNIVERSITY OF CHICAGO PRESS

Supplementary Educational Monographs

PUBLISHED IN CONJUNCTION WITH *The School Review*
AND *The Elementary School Journal*

NUMBER 78 · JUNE 1953

THE UNIVERSITY OF CHICAGO PRESS, CHICAGO 37
Cambridge University Press, London, N.W. 1, England

*Copyright 1953 by The University of Chicago. All rights
reserved. Published 1953. Composed and printed by* THE
UNIVERSITY OF CHICAGO PRESS, *Chicago, Illinois, U.S.A.*

0.5
fs
78

BF
721
B66

PREFACE

This is the second of a series of reports on the work
of a Community Youth Development Program sponsored by the
Committee on Human Development of the University of Chicago.
The first report was published a year ago as Number 1 in the
Youth Development Series, Supplementary Educational Monographs, Number 75. It told of the beginning of the project
in September, 1951, and described the general design and
plan to be followed. The present monograph will report on
the first full year of operation and the beginning of the
second year. Since this report is written in January, a
complete report on the second year will have to be given in
later publications.

The first year was devoted to studying the children of
the community and to training people in the community for
work on the project. The second year has seen the start of
real work with children. The work with children was bound
to bring us down to reality--to expose some of the major
difficulties and to test our preparation to meet them.

Thus this second report is a sober, down-to-earth account of what we did, why we did it, what difficulties we
met, and how we tried to overcome them. There are no results to report yet, since we have just begun to work with
children. We cannot hope for anything definite in the way
of results on the experimental group of children for at
least five years.

This volume is intended for those who are interested
in the techniques that we are using in studying and working
with children and parents.

The research committee of faculty members from the University of Chicago which works with the project consists of:

John M. Butler, assistant professor of psychology and
    counselor

Frank T. Flynn, Jr., associate professor of social-
    service administration

Robert J. Havighurst, professor of education and chair-
    man of the Committee on Human Development

Maurice F. Seay, professor and chairman, Department of
    Education

Ross Snyder, associate professor, Federated Theological Faculty

Ralph W. Tyler, professor of education and dean of the Division of Social Sciences

W. Lloyd Warner, professor of anthropology and sociology

We wish to acknowledge the interest and assistance of the Moorman Foundation, which has supplied us with the funds necessary for the project and which has also made it possible for the local school board to extend the screening program for talent and for maladjustment which we commenced last year, to the next two fourth-grade classes.

ROBERT J. HAVIGHURST

The University of Chicago

TABLE OF CONTENTS

TABLE OF CONTENTS

PART IV

THE COMMUNITY

LIST OF TABLES

LIST OF TABLES

CHAPTER 1

A REVIEW OF THE FIRST YEAR
OF THE PROJECT

The Motivating Needs

The general motivation for a project such as the Community Youth Development Program[1] springs from the growing national concern for the conservation and development of our human resources, especially the conservation of mental health and the development of talent. The cost of mental ill health is much larger than the country can afford; approximately half the hospital beds of the nation are occupied by mental patients, and an estimated 50 per cent or more of general medical cases have psychological components. In addition, there is great concern about the heavy cost of crime and juvenile delinquency, the loss to industry from inept dealing with employees and their problems of human relations, and the high cost of adequate education of children for citizenship in a democracy. Finally, the nation is beginning to realize the great loss to the world that occurs through failure to recognize and develop talents and abilities that exist in many persons unknown to themselves and others.

The more specific motivation for this project stemmed from a seven-year observational study of the personal and social development of youth in a Midwestern community recently completed by members of the Committee on Human Development at the University of Chicago. Those working with this study found themselves observing signs of maladjustment and signs of talent in young people, frequently saw the maladjustment develop into serious social problems and the talent go undeveloped, but, because of the observational nature of the study, were not empowered to attempt remedial action.

---

[1]For a detailed description of the initiation of the project, see Robert J. Havighurst, Robert F. DeHaan, William J. Dieterich, Henry Hackamack, LaVona Johnson, and Robert D. King, A Community Youth Development Program. Youth Development Series, No. 1. Supplementary Educational Monographs, No. 75. Chicago: University of Chicago Press, 1952.

At this point it was resolved to undertake as soon as possible an experimental project which not only would discover potential talent and emotional maladjustment but would be aimed at a developmental and preventive program for those individuals in need of it.

The project was to emphasize the early discovery of symptoms of maladjustment so that many children could be given help that might prevent their becoming serious problems. Early discovery of special talents of children would make possible their fuller development through the provision of information, opportunities, and additional training.

Available Resources

While the need is great, the community facilities for help in these areas are usually inadequate. Most of the existing agencies are doing effective work, regardless of their particular name or theoretical orientation, but, as a rule, their budgets and staffs are totally inadequate. Clinics of all kinds (mental-hygiene clinics, counseling centers, child-guidance clinics, psychological clinics, marriage counselors, etc.) can point to a high degree of success in helping their clients to more effective and happy living. Such services need to be greatly expanded, but there are certain problems that the clinics will always have difficulty in meeting. For instance, the clinics that exist are reaching only a small per cent of the people needing services. Many of these persons do not seek help because of lack of knowledge of clinic services, because of misconceptions about their use, and because of fear of asking for help; and the clinic itself usually has no means of discovering or making contact with those persons needing help who do not take the initiative in seeking professional assistance. Again, clinics exist in relatively few communities, and the supply of adequately trained professional persons is so limited that many communities cannot rely upon the possibility of establishing clinic services for many years to come. Nevertheless, at the present time clinics and practicing clinicians are our major resources for the improvement of mental health.

Other sources for professional help are the specially trained counselors attached to the staffs of various institutions in the community, such as industries, schools, hos-

pitals, or courts. While the number of such positions is
increasing, they face the same limitations as do the clinics.

A largely untapped resource is that group of persons
found in every community who are concerned about problems
of human development and who work with people in personal
and professional ways, but who are relatively untrained in
psychological areas. Many people are directly involved,
such as public school teachers, nurses, social-welfare agency personnel, Scout Leaders, Sunday School teachers and re-
ligious workers, recreation and other group workers. They
are aware of the needs of youth, they have daily contact
with the young people, and they usually welcome some help
in meeting these developmental needs, but they have not
often had training in the techniques that they require to
be of maximum usefulness.

The Hypothesis

This background of thinking led the Committee on Human
Development at the University of Chicago to form a research
committee to plan and initiate an experimental program designed to throw light on questions such as these: What can
communities do to help prevent, or to solve, the personal
and social problems of their children? How can existing
research knowledge and clinically developed techniques be
made available to local communities in a usable form? Can
a youth development program be devised, the operation of
which will rely mainly on residents in the community and
require a minimum of expenditure of funds?

Obviously, such questions can best be explored in an
action-research project in an actual community setting, and
the research committee undertook to design such a program.

The basic, general hypothesis might be stated in the
following terms: An average American community with its own
resources of persons and finances can significantly improve
the mental-health level and the extent of the use of the
talent of its citizens when interested persons in the community are given information and training in scientific methods of human development.

The Design

To test this general hypothesis the following design
was formulated for the experimental project:

1.   The experimental group would include all children in
the fourth grade of the public schools in the beginning
year of the project. The control group would include
all children in the sixth grade of the public schools
in the same beginning year.

2.   A battery of tests would be given to both experimental
and control groups during the first project year to
discover potential maladjustment in the children and
the presence of special talents.

3.   A staff of volunteer counselors from the local community would be selected and given a course of training.
They would then be divided into counseling teams that
would work with individual children.

4.   Those children of the experimental group who scored
highest in potential maladjustment and highest in special talents would make up the case loads of counseling teams, who would study the children further and
then, from their own membership and from the community
at large, muster all the aid possible to assist the
children's development. Children in the control group
would be given no special help other than that which
the community would ordinarily have offered.

5.   The experimental group would be studied and assisted
for ten years by the counseling teams. Identical
records on individual children and their development
would be kept for both experimental and control groups.

6.   At the end of ten years, the experimental and the control groups would be compared on all possible measures
indicative of the mental health and talent development
of the two groups. Some of these would be: delinquency
rate, divorce rate, academic progress, school drop-outs,
per cent of the groups going to college, employment
records, creative and artistic productions, etc.

7.   Further evaluation of the project would be made by
assessing the changes in the community itself and in
the programs of the various agencies that could legit-
imately be attributed wholly or partially to the work

of the project. Changes in the programs of the individual agencies, development of new or different methods of work, the increase of co-operative efforts between agencies, community demand for additional services, increasing use of existing services, additions
to staff, and improvement in the training level of
staff persons—all would be indexes of general community
change. However, in order to determine the role of the
project in producing such changes, these measures might
have to be compared with the youth-serving programs of
neighboring cities.

Initiation of the Project

In January, 1951, a representative of **the** University
of Chicago arrived in a Midwestern community of forty-two
thousand people to present the idea of this project. During the next three months the project was explained to many
civic leaders and most local social and educational organizations. It was stated that the project would not require
expenditure of funds by the local community but would require the expenditure of time and effort by many persons.
The University advisory committee also met with representatives of local groups on several occasions. A Steering
Committee was formed that undertook further to sound out
local organizations, and, if the sentiment was favorable,
to establish a Community Youth Development Commission. The
University advisory committee undertook to seek funds to
support the project. The Steering Committee succeeded in
formally establishing the Commission in July, 1951.

The Commission was composed of persons of the community interested in youth who were named as representatives
to the Commission by their parent organizations. Nineteen
civic, welfare, and educational organizations named representatives to this first meeting, and that number has since
been expanded to twenty-five. The Commission appointed a
Professional Committee made up of professional youth workers from those organizations represented on the Commission.
The original group of eleven such workers has now expanded
to fourteen members.

Finally, the operating staff was formed when the Commission named an executive secretary from the community and

the University of Chicago named three consultants from its
staff.   This team began work in September, 1951, in a down-
town office building, nine months after the original discussions began.

This over-all picture of the project has necessarily
been given in brief outline, but further details can be obtained from the 1952 monograph. The accompanying chart represents the organizational relationships of the project.   The
Community Youth Development Commission, made up of representatives of the boards of community agencies, is the major policy-making group. The Professional Committee, created by the
Commission, has general concern with the technical aspects of
the project. The nine teams of counselors were selected
through the efforts of the Professional Committee, and their
problems are now brought to the Professional Committee. The
Talent Committees were formed in a similar manner, and now
operate fairly independently in an effort to screen the
children for talents in the fine arts.

The operating staff is composed of consultants from
the University of Chicago and the executive secretary appointed by the Commission.   The staff members carry out the
administrative work of the project and serve as consultants
and advisers to all groups associated with the Commission.

Specific Activities of First Year

After the completion of the organization of the project,
the first task was to discover and select persons in the community to make up the volunteer staff on whom would fall the
task of working with children through teams.   Mainly through
the efforts of the Professional Committee, seventy-five persons were brought together and given a year's course, two
hours a week, on child development and skills related to
working with children.

A second major activity was the selection and the administration of a battery of tests to all children in the fourth
grade (experimental group) and the sixth grade (control group.

The third major activity was to discover those persons
in the community who were most interested in the development
of the fine arts and to organize them into functional committees.

All these activities were begun in the first year and
carried over into the second year's work.

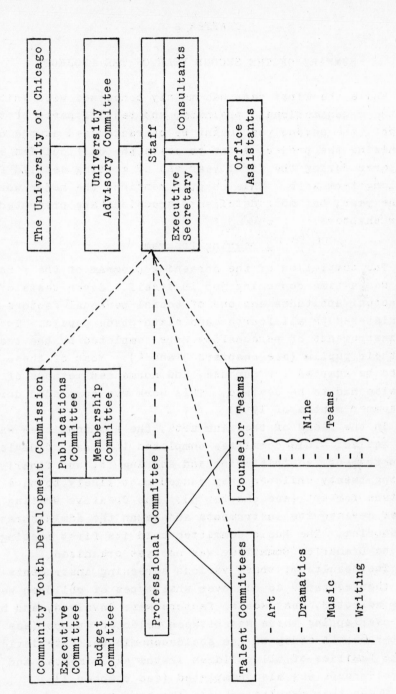

Fig. 1.—Organizational Chart of the
Community Youth Development Program

CHAPTER 2

SUMMARY OF THE SECOND YEAR OF THE PROJECT

While the first year was mainly concerned with initiating the organizational, training, and testing parts of the project, the second year might be characterized as one of organizing the project so as to solve the difficulties encountered during the first year and of getting settled for the long-term work. This chapter mentions the major work of the year, but more detailed discussions are presented in later chapters.

Screening Program

The completion of the screening program of the first year was a time-consuming job in itself. Seven tests of intellectual aptitudes and one of social-personal factors were administered to all fourth- and sixth-grade pupils. Two rating instruments of personality were completed by the teachers for their pupils (see chapters 3 and 4). Most of these tests had to be adapted for our use, and norms and methods of scoring also had to be devised. This work was completed during the summer months of 1952.

In the field of the fine arts, the Art Committee was most active. This committee completed its task of devising an instrument, administering and scoring it, and finally selecting twenty children they judged most likely to have an aptitude for art (see chapter 5). The Creative Writing Committee devised its instruments and began the administration and scoring. The Music Committee held its first meetings, but the Dramatics Committee was not yet organized.

The results of these various screening instruments were then compared to discover what types of children were being selected, what social factors were involved, and how much overlapping there was between selected groups (see chapter 6). A study of the socioeconomic characteristics of the families of all children in the experimental and the control groups was also completed (see chapter 7).

These test results provide the base from which to work with individual children, and they will be used in later re-

8

search studies. Other testing will be done in the future
with these and other instruments, but the testing will not
be so extensive as it has been during the past year.

Treatment Program

The central interest of the project is the selection,
training, and functioning of teams of local people to help
children. The first general course of training was completed in May, 1952 (see chapter 8), and it has been partially
evaluated here. At the same time, individual teams of six
to eight members each were formed, and some training sessions were held before the summer (chapter 9).

In September, the entire group met in a general seminar.
The work of the individual teams was then picked up after
the lapse of the summer vacation period. Ten selected children were assigned to each team, and they began their work
in different ways (see chapter 10). In the beginning, se-
vere difficulties arose which seriously handicapped their
effectiveness, and three new activities were developed to
help meet the difficulties. A play-therapy room and an observation room were set up to help provide referral sources
for professional treatment of disturbed children, as well
as to offer further training to a number of the team members and other professional workers of the community (see
chapter 12).

It was originally assumed that the teams would not be
in direct contact with the children or their parents, that
in most cases families would be unaware of team activities.
It was also expected that some report of the test results
would be offered to the parents. These two ideas were modified through an activity aimed at bringing the parents more
directly into the project and at providing a point of contact between teams and parents. For this purpose, the parents of all tested children were interviewed to report test
results, to discuss concerns about the child, and to discuss plans for things that could be done for him. This
idea was tried out experimentally in one school in November,
1952, and was afterward extended to other schools (chapter 12).

In September, when children were assigned to the teams,
it was the judgment of team members that the assignments

should be made in some arbitrary fashion. As a result each
team had both talented and disturbed children, children from
many schools, boys and girls. This procedure led to many
difficulties, and, after much investigation, the case loads
were completely reorganized so that all the children selected from one or two schools would be assigned to one team.
This reorganization was completed in December, 1952 (chapter 11).

At this writing the intensive work of teams with selected children is in its first stages, and results cannot be expected for some time to come. In one sense this stage is one
of the most difficult, in that the initial enthusiasm of
starting a new effort has somewhat decreased, while the sat-
isfaction of observed results has not yet begun.

PART I.--STUDY OF GIFTED AND OF
EMOTIONALLY DISTURBED CHILDREN

CHAPTER 3

SCREENING FOR INTELLECTUAL APTITUDES

In selecting gifted children, it was obvious that we
should be interested in those with the greatest intellectual aptitudes. For the reasons that are summarized in the
following paragraphs, we used several tests to measure in-
tellect.

General Considerations on
Intelligence Testing

There are a number of different kinds of intellectual
ability, which are called "primary mental abilities." Different tests must be used to measure these different abilities. In addition, there is a kind of "general" intelligence, which is measured by certain tests. Furthermore,
there are abilities that are directly related to success in
one occupation or another, such as scientific ability and
mechanical ability.

Some people show high abilities in a number of intellectual areas. They may be said to be consistently superior.
Other people have great ability in only one or two areas and
are average or even low in other areas. They show what may
be called specialized superiority. Thus we may expect to
find two groups of children, those showing consistent superiority and those showing specialized superiority.

Young children do not show as many different mental
abilities as they will in adolescence. Hence, it is best
with younger children to use tests of general intelligence
as well as tests of such primary mental abilities as have
been discovered in children of that age.

The fact that our tests are not equally valid for all
groups of children also qualifies our screening procedure.
Aptitude tests include problems that are not equally familiar or unfamiliar to all groups of children. For instance,
a test of vocabulary knowledge for younger children usually
includes, for its more difficult items, words like banquet
and symphony, which a child of middle-class parents is more
likely to have learned in the home than is a child of work-

ing-class parents. Accordingly, efforts must be made to secure tests which are, as nearly as possible, equally "fair"
to various socioeconomic groups, to rural as well as urban
children, and so on. If such tests cannot be obtained, the
results on the tests which are given should be interpreted
in the light of these probable shortcomings. (Children of
underprivileged families might be given a supplement to
their test scores to make up for the probable bias of the
test against them.)

Choosing the Tests

Since the schools of the city were giving routinely
the SRA Primary Mental Abilities test in the fourth grade,
scores on this test were used in the screening procedure.
The total score, computed as advised in the test manual, was
used as a measure of general intelligence. In addition, the
scores on separate primary mental abilities which are measured by this test were available for use.

As a test of "mother-wit" which might be relatively independent of socioeconomic status, the Davis-Eells Games
were used. This test, published by the World Book Company,
is administered by the classroom teacher without requiring
the children to read anything. The test items consist en-
tirely of pictures or picture sequences, and the administrator reads the directions, asking the pupils to mark their
answers in appropriate blanks on the side of the page of the
test booklet. The problems require the same mental processes as are required by problems in group tests which involve
reading, such as drawing inferences, grasping analogies,
recognizing absurdities, solving everyday problems around
the house and neighborhood, changing money. It is intended that all the problems be equally familiar or unfamiliar
to the various socioeconomic or racial groups which take
the test. This test gives a single score of general intelligence.

Another measure of general intelligence was the Goodenough Draw-a-Man test. As is well known, this test is less
closely related to socioeconomic status than are most tests,
although it is not a "culture-free" test. This was given as
part of an artistic aptitude test, and the drawings were used
both for the assessment of artistic aptitude and for the
assessment of intelligence.

Certain tests of specific mental abilities were also
given, for two reasons. It was expected that they would
serve as a beginning of a search for children with specialized talents. Five such tests were given during the year,
and others will be given in the future. Another reason for
giving these tests was to get tests that would have a high
ceiling for this group and thus differentiate more clearly
among the gifted children. For this reason, tests that are
ordinarily used with older children were given to this
group. Three of the intermediate-level SRA Primary Mental
Abilities tests (2) were given--those for the abilities of
V (verbal meaning), S (space), and R (reasoning). Two other tests of specific abilities were used, the Street Gestalt
test, which is a good measure of Thurstone's C_1, or first
closure factor, and the Concealed Figures test, developed by
Thurstone as a measure of his C_2, or second closure factor.
These tests were included because it was thought that they
might have some relationship to creativity, a quality which
will be explored in several ways in the project.

Administering the Tests

The SRA Primary Mental Abilities test, Form AH, was administered to all fourth-graders and scored by the classroom
teachers, as part of the regular testing program in the
schools. The teachers were instructed in giving and scoring
the test by a supervisor who did a careful job of training.
Nevertheless, some mistakes crept into this work. On two of
the tests, those for P (perception) and N (number ability),
the time allowed must be watched carefully, since most pupils will improve their scores if given more than the allotted time. The unusually high scores of a few classes on
these tests gave evidence that the time limits had not been
observed accurately. Consequently, these particular sub-
tests were dropped out of the scoring in those classes. A
few mistakes were made in scoring, but these were caught by
checking the scoring on the test booklets.

The Davis-Eells Games, Elementary Form A, 1952, was
used with the fourth- and sixth-graders. This test requires
the administrator to read every problem from a practice manual to the pupils, so that they will not need to read while
taking the test. The classroom teachers administered this

test to most of the children, although a supervisor or some
other trained person substituted for the teacher in a few
classes. All the test administrators met to go over this
test with the supervisor. The directions require them to
start the test with an opening game in which the children
would develop a set toward the test as if it were a game
that all children can play well. The test was called a
"game" always. The teachers reported unanimously that the
children enjoyed the "game" and called for more. In the
sixth grades a few teachers dispensed with the opening
"game" (the familiar exercise of rubbing the stomach with
one hand while patting the head with the other hand), saying that it made them feel foolish to do this game and their
pupils knew it was a test anyway. Probably this was not a
serious drawback in the case of the sixth-graders. More serious was the fact that the test had a low ceiling for sixth-
graders, and thus there was not good discrimination among
those who scored high in this grade. For fourth-graders the
test gave a good range and distribution of scores.

The Draw-a-Man test was given with standard instructions except that the pupil was asked to draw a person.
Consequently, a number of children drew women, and the scoring system had to be adapted slightly for these drawings.

The V, S, and R tests of the Intermediate Form of the
Primary Mental Abilities tests were administered as follows:

| | Time Limit (Number of Minutes) | |
Test	This Adminis-tration	Regular Adminis-tration
Verbal meaning:		
Vocabulary	8	4
Completion	10	6
Space:		
Figures	8	5
Cards	8	5
Reasoning:		
Letter Series	8	6
Letter Grouping	6	4

Since these tests are designed for use in the age range
11-17 while our subjects were aged 9-11, it seemed wise to
extend the time limits. Consequently, the test became more

of a power test and less of a speed test. This was especially true in the verbal-meaning tests, where practically
all the children quit before the time was up because they
had reached words with which they were completely unfamiliar. The items on these tests are fairly well graded in
difficulty, with the easier ones first. In the space test
there is little or no gradation in difficulty, and most of
the children worked through the entire time allotted them
but without finishing the test. In the reasoning tests
there is a gradation of difficulty, and no pupil finished
the test in the time allotted, while a number gave up before the end of the time because of the difficulty of the
items reached. In general, then, these tests did measure
the limits of the abilities of these children in their respective areas, and the high ceiling allowed the ablest
children to demonstrate their superiority unequivocally.

The Street Gestalt Completion test was given with a
ten-minute time limit, and few of the children finished.
This test consists of black-and-white reproductions of familiar figures and objects, with varying amounts of these
figures blocked out (3). The problem is to see what the
whole figure or Gestalt is and to write the name of the object below the figure. Children of this age range have little difficulty in perceiving objects in the test, although
many of their perceptions may be inaccurate. Their main
difficulty is in spelling the words they write below the
picture. Consequently, there were always two or three persons in the room to help with spelling. Children were instructed to raise their hands when they needed help. They
whispered the word to the supervisor, who whispered the
correct spelling to them.

The Thurstone Concealed Figures test (Form A, 1950) is
an adaptation of the Gottschaldt Figures test, which requires the subject to look at a series of geometrical figures and to decide which of those in a series of four figures contain a more or less simple key figure shown at the
left of the series. There are forty-nine items or series
of figures, not ordered as to difficulty.

This test has been used by Thurstone and others with
men in the armed services, with college students, and with
high-school students. We found that it could be given to

fourth- and sixth-graders but that the directions must be given carefully. The practice period was 10-15 minutes. The practice figures were drawn in chalk on a blackboard, and often colored chalk was used to outline the key figure concealed in the test items. Under these conditions practically all the children grasped the problem, although there were a few zero scores. A time limit of ten minutes was allowed, and none of the children completed the test.

These five tests of specific mental abilities were given in three sittings, none lasting over thirty-five minutes. They were given in the following blocks: (1) verbal meaning and space tests of the Primary Mental Abilities tests; (2) C_1 of the Gestalt Completion and the reasoning test of the Primary Mental Abilities; and (3) C_2 measured by the Concealed Figures test. These tests were given by experienced test administrators, each with an assistant, and in groups of ordinary class size. In some schools not all the children in the fourth and sixth grades were tested with these five tests. Children whose intelligence scores were below 95 on the elementary Primary Mental Abilities tests and the Davis-Eells Games were omitted from the testing in the larger schools. However, a complete range of ability was tested because all children in the smaller schools were tested.

Scoring the Tests

The tests were scored and the raw scores handled as follows:

Elementary Primary Mental Abilities.--The raw scores were transformed to intelligence quotients by the method advised in the Test Manual.

Davis-Eells Games.--The raw scores were plotted against age, and an age correction was determined. All fourth-grade scores were corrected to the median age for fourth-graders, and all sixth-grade scores were corrected to the median age for sixth-graders. The age-corrected scores were then turned into intelligence-quotient equivalents by equating the mean Davis-Eells score for each grade to an index score of 101 and using 8 points on the Davis-Eells scale (the standard deviation was 8 points) as equivalent to 16 points on the intelligence-quotient scale. This procedure was based on the fact that the intelligence-quotient scores on the

Primary Mental Abilities test had a mean of 101 and a standard deviation of 15. Therefore the Davis-Eells converted score was made equal to 101 plus twice the deviation of that score from its mean.

Draw-a-Man.--The usual scoring procedure produced a mean intelligence quotient of 100 on the Draw-a-Man test for fourth-graders, with a standard deviation of 18. The drawings were scored by several persons. In order to check the reliability of their scores, all at first scored the same drawings and discussed their differences until they arrived at common procedures. Inter-scorer correlations were of the order of .97. In drawings of women or girls, it was noted that the presence of skirts in the drawing made it difficult to tell whether the hip joint was shown correctly, which is one of the fifty-one points used in scoring the drawing. A judgment was made on the basis of the parts of the legs which were showing. It was also impossible sometimes to tell whether to give credit for drawing ears correctly, since in some drawings of women the ears were obscured by hair. Since there are two possible points of credit for ears, these drawings were allowed one point if hair covered the places where ears should be. This may have penalized a few of the minority of children who drew pictures of women.

Another difficulty with the Draw-a-Man test was in the scoring of drawings of sixth-graders. This test is not supposed to be suitable for children above the sixth-grade level, and its ceiling is thought to be low even for this level. The age norms given by Goodenough run up to 14.5 (raw score 42 out of a maximum of 51, and increasing at the rate of 4 points a year). Thus for a child aged 11.5, the effective ceiling of the intelligence quotient would be 125. We extrapolated the age norms to 16.0 (score 48), which gave us a maximum intelligence quotient of almost 140, a point reached by one sixth-grader. Two attained intelligence quotients of 133, and a good number between 120 and 131. Compared with the fourth-graders, these results indicate something of a ceiling effect, for there were five fourth-graders with intelligence quotients over 140 on the Draw-a-Man test, and thirteen with intelligence quotients over 130. The mean sixth-grade intelligence quotient was 101, with a standard deviation of 16.8.

Primary Mental Abilities: Verbal meaning, space, and reasoning.--There are no age norms for children as young as nine or ten on the V, S, and R tests, and as the time limits were lengthened over those stipulated in the Test Manual, the age norms for sixth-graders were inapplicable. Consequently, the raw scores on these tests were corrected for age differences by computing an age-correction factor from the age norms given in the Scoring and Interpretation Manual, The Chicago Tests of Primary Mental Abilities, Ages 11 to 17. Although this required extrapolation of these age norms, the extrapolations were not extensive, and the magnitude of the age corrections was never great enough to cause any major error. The age-corrected scores were then turned into percentile scores for each grade group and were used in that form.

Street Gestalt Completion test (C_1).--In the original work with this test Street found no substantial change with age in the age range 9-11, and our results confirmed this finding (r=.04 for raw score and age in the fourth grade, and r=.02 for raw score and age in the sixth grade). The scoring procedure for the Street Gestalt test was modified from that used by Street. In his method each right answer was scored 1, and each wrong answer 0. But there are a number of fairly popular answers to several of the pictures which are almost, but not quite, correct. For instance, there is a picture of a baby which can easily be taken for a circus clown, and one of a baseball pitcher which can be easily perceived as a football player who has just made a forward pass. Consequently, a scoring key was constructed which allowed 2 points for the "correct" answer, and, for a small number of drawings, 1 point for a fairly accurate perception. It is doubtful that this method offered any great improvement over that of Street. One small advantage was that it widened the distribution of scores at the high end of the scale, where a relatively large number of scores were clustered close together with Street's method. The raw scores were transformed into percentile scores.

Concealed Figures (C_2).--This test was scored by subtracting wrong answers from right answers. Since there was a considerable age change, an age correction was determined by comparing median scores for each quarter-year age group.

The age correction was one point per quarter-year. The age-corrected scores were transformed to percentile scores for each grade group.

Selection of Gifted Children

The simplest method of selecting the children with intellectual talent is to make a composite score by combining the several test scores, and to rank the children by means of these composite scores. This was done, by adding the three intelligence-quotients scores for the Elementary Primary Mental Abilities test, the Davis-Eells Games, and the Draw-a-Man tests, to five percentile scores--V, S, R, C_2 and the combined C_1 plus C_2 score turned into a percentile score. The reasons for this particular combination were as follows: Using percentile scores for V, S, R, C_2 and (C_1+C_2) gave each of these scores less weight than that of an intelligence-quotient score, which had a higher value for a given relative position (an intelligence quotient of 100 equals a percentile of 50); this seems justifiable because the V, S, R, C_1 and C_2 are specialized factor scores, while the other three are more general scores of intelligence. The C_1 score alone did not appear to the staff to justify as much weight as the others. It has almost a zero correlation with the other test scores and has not been found to be related to any significant mental ability. In fact, we had some question about including it at all, but we concluded that it would be useful for further study. C_1 is thus combined with C_2 and gets only half as much weight as the other special-ability tests. C_2, in turn, gets more weight than the other tests. This is supported by our feeling that C_2 is a more significant mental ability than some of the others.

This method of forming a composite score is certainly crude and will be improved as we get more information. But we have no information at present that would justify some other set of weights, and any small modification of the weights would make little or no change in the rankings of the high-level children. The present scoring system will probably be revised and made more sophisticated after another year or two of experience.

The children in the fourth and sixth grades were ranked in order of their composite-test scores to make a roster of

those who show <u>consistent superiority</u>. This consists of all
children who are above the ninetieth percentile in three or
more of the eight tests, and at the fortieth percentile or
higher in all the others.

On the other hand, there is a group who may be said to
show <u>specialized superiority</u>, who are very high in one or
two tests but below the ninetieth percentile in all other
tests. A roster was made of those children, including all
who were at the ninety-eighth or ninety-ninth percentile in
one or two tests and below the ninetieth percentile in all
others. Some of the children dropped as low as the fifth
or tenth percentile in some tests. For instance, several
were very high in S and very low in V.

Thus two groups of intellectually superior children
were selected: those with <u>consistent superiority</u>, and those
with <u>specialized superiority</u>. It is expected that those
with specialized superiority will show relatively greater
problems of social and emotional adjustment.

More girls than boys in the groups showed consistent
superiority. The ratio of girls to boys is almost two to
one in the fourth grade, and nearly as high in the sixth
grade. On the other hand, the boys outnumber the girls
slightly in the group showing specialized superiority.

Intercorrelations of Test Scores

Table 1 shows the intercorrelations of the various
test scores for boys and girls in the fourth and sixth
grades. This table also shows correlations of test scores
with socioeconomic status (ISC). No special comments will
be made on these correlations at the present time. They
will be used in the selection of tests for screening children in subsequent years and for the study and interpretation of talent as we secure more data on other kinds of
talent and on changes with age.

TABLE 1

Intercorrelations* between Tests Used for Screening
Fourth-Grade and Sixth-Grade Boys (above Diagonal
Lines) and Girls (below Diagonal Lines)

Tests	Socioeconomic Status	Primary Mental Abilities	Davis-Eells Games	Draw-a-Man	Verbal Meaning	Space	Reasoning	Closure$_1$	Closure$_2$
Fourth Grade									
Socioeconomic status .		.39	.34	.17	.34	.24	.29	.22	.34
Primary Mental Abilities	.43		.55	.31	...	...	...	.33	.45
Davis-Eells Games . .	.37	.65		.42	.29	.39	.48	.28	.36
Draw-a-Man	.15	.50	.43		.10	.43	.31	.21	.54
Verbal meaning	.26	...	.41	.31		.13	.28	.35	.20
Space	.22	...	.40	.28	.26		.43	.20	.50
Reasoning	.38	...	.45	.31	.50	.47		.27	.38
Closure$_1$	.20	.22	.17	.09	.24	.09	.09		.19
Closure$_2$	.30	.57	.45	.45	.32	.53	.53	.12	
Sixth Grade									
Socioeconomic status .		.49	.30	.17	.33	.26	.21	.11	.14
Primary Mental Abilities	.34		.61	.32	.57	.51	.52	.32	.43
Davis-Eells Games . .	.19	.58		.42	.56	.47	.58	.33	.51
Draw-a-Man	.23	.57	.59		.37	.33	.27	.31	.42
Verbal meaning	.24	.49	.35	.43		.42	.55	.33	.37
Space	.16	.45	.51	.54	.31		.55	.15	.50
Reasoning	.25	.53	.54	.58	.53	.59		.26	.58
Closure$_1$	.02	.26	.34	.23	.29	.15	.27		.26
Closure$_2$	.25	.59	.54	.52	.50	.57	.64	.21	

*All the correlation coefficients are positive, except
those involving the socioeconomic index, which are all negative. A high index means low socioeconomic status.

Bibliography

1. Davis, Allison, and Eells, Kenneth W. Davis-Eells Games.
   Yonkers-on-Hudson, New York: World Book Co., 1953.

2. Goodenough, Florence L. <u>Measuring Intelligence by Means
   of Drawings</u>. Yonkers-on-Hudson, New York: World Book
   Co., 1926.

3. Street, Roy F. A Gestalt Completion Test. New York:
   Bureau of Publications, Teachers College, Columbia University, 1931.

4. Thurstone, L. L. Concealed Figures Test, Form A, 1950.

5. Thurstone, L. L., and Thurstone, Thelma Gwinn. SRA
   Primary Mental Abilities for Ages 7 to 11, Elementary
   Form: <u>Examiner Manual</u>. Chicago: Science Research Asso-
   ciates, 1948.

6. Thurstone, L. L., and Thurstone, Thelma Gwinn. SRA
   Primary Mental Abilities for Ages 11 to 17, Intermedi-
   ate form AH (separate test edition). Chicago: Science
   Research Associates, 1941.

CHAPTER 4

SCREENING FOR MALADJUSTMENT AND FOR LEADERSHIP

Two aspects of youth development which are of obvious importance to individuals and to their communities are the achievement of an adequate social and emotional adjustment and the ability to function in a leadership role. So that special help in these areas may be most efficiently applied, it is desirable to find ways of identifying those children who can be expected to have the most difficulty in adjustment and those children who have the most to offer as leaders.

In the area of maladjustment, two dimensions were conceptualized, which might be described generally as "aggressive maladjustment" and "withdrawn" or "passive maladjustment." For social leadership, one general dimension was conceived as adequate for use at the elementary-school age level.

Within the setting of the Community Youth Development Program, certain demands were made upon any program of screening for these characteristics. Since the experimental and the control groups totaled some seven hundred children, instruments designed for mass application were obviously indicated. Efficiency in administration and scoring was a requisite. Because of the size of the group, it was necessary to have a fairly large number of people sharing the labor of the screening program. These requirements suggested the use of instruments that would make possible a comparative evaluation of children through objectification of the observations of people who were familiar with the pupils' overt behavior and traits of personality. Two groups of persons were especially available as judges: the teachers and the age mates of the subjects.

Two instruments were developed, the Behavior Description Chart, for use by teachers and other adults, and a Guess-Who Test, for use by children. Because both maladjustment and leadership were to be predicted upon the basis of observation of overt behavior, items relating to these

23

traits were combined in these screening instruments. In the area of maladjustment, the theoretical orientation and findings of Hewitt and Jenkins (2, 3, 4) provided the basis for selection of specific items. In the area of social leadership, both specific behaviors of the subject and responses of others to him which would seem to indicate the performance of a leadership function were hypothesized to be useful items predicting eventual capacity for adult leadership.

The Behavior Description Chart

The main problem which was faced in using adults' observations as a resource in screening for maladjustment and leadership was making the data from one judge comparable to those of another judge. For the experimental group twenty judges were involved, with no more than one judge being used for any given child.

In this case the ratings made by one individual for a specific child must be compared with the ratings made on another child by a second individual. Thus, there is a great possibility for variation between judges, not only in the standards of leniency or severity which the judge applies to the instrument, but, in the case of many rating instruments, in the range of behavior in the group of children which serves as a frame of reference for the judge in making quantitative judgments on the presence or absence of a trait In the Behavior Description Chart the attempt was made to reduce such inter-judge variations by having the judge compare traits of personality and behavior with other such traits of the same individual without reference to his group and without direct quantitative evaluation.

An example of one of the items of the Behavior Description Chart is the following:

1. A. Others come to him for help.
   B. Causes disturbances.
   C. Is easily irritated, flustered, or upset.
   D. Reports those who break the rules.
   E. Shows emotions in a restrained way.

There are eighteen of these pentads, or five-statement items, in the instrument, which is given in full in Appendix G. For each of these pentads the judge is instructed to select the one statement which is most like the subject

child and the one statement which is <u>least like</u> the child.
In the five items of each pentad one of the statements is
descriptive of social leadership (A in the example given
above), one of aggressive maladjustment (B, above), and one
of withdrawn maladjustment (C, above). The two remaining
statements are more nearly neutral in tone and might easily
be attributed to an "average" child, for whom none of the
three significant statements seems appropriate. The two
neutral statements are included in order that the judge may
not be forced to throw the child into one of the three special groups.

In some respects the Behavior Description Chart resem-
bles a forced-choice instrument (5). Characteristic of the
forced-choice instrument is the use of pairs or groups of
favorable and of unfavorable items, the members of a pair
having equal rater-preference value but unequal discrimina-
tion-value. Items A and E above, for example, are items of
nearly equal rater-preference value; teachers are about
equally disposed to use one or the other of them in rating
children. Items B, C, and D, also, have approximately
equal rater-preference value. In terms of discrimination
value, however, Item A clearly favors well-adjusted children who have some leadership qualities, while Item E does
not. Similarly, Items B and C select children who are maladjusted, while Item D does not.

The Behavior Description Chart thus gives the judge
or rater an opportunity to rate a given child as <u>most like</u>
and as <u>least like</u> any of five items, of which one is predictive of leadership, one of aggressive maladjustment, one
of withdrawn maladjustment, and two are not predictive of
either good or poor adjustment. A score can then be obtained for each child on each of the three types of good
or poor adjustment in which we are interested. The instrument is designed to overcome some of the tendency of a particular judge to rate children favorably or unfavorably,
by putting in a number of favorable or slightly negative
items which may be attractive to a judge, and which do accurately describe many "average" children, but which do not
count toward the child's score. Thus, only the children
who seem to the judges to be especially well or especially
poorly adjusted should get high scores on these character-

istics. The "average" child should be rated as most like
many of the nondiscriminating statements.

Choice of items for the Behavior Description Chart.--
The items on the Behavior Description Chart have come mainly from behavior check lists which have been used by the
Committee on Human Development of the University of Chicago
and others. The principal source of items was the check
list which had been used in a study of moral character (1).
Many of the statements on this check list deal with friend-
liness, loyalty, kindness, honesty, and self-control. Ullmann (6), in devising a behavior-rating instrument for mental-hygiene purposes, used this reservoir of descriptive
statements, added others to it, and created a forced-choice
rating instrument that was predictive of good and poor adjustment in children of the later elementary-school grades.
Ullmann sent us his list of items, with their rater-preference values and discrimination values. He determined the
discrimination value of the items by asking teachers to apply his instrument to children of their acquaintance who
were very well adjusted or very poorly adjusted. He also
asked psychiatrists to rate the items for their presumed
discrimination value. Thus, his criterion of discrimination for the items indicative of poor adjustment was that
they should be applied to children with an over-all poor
adjustment. He did not attempt to separate items indicative of aggressive maladjustment from those indicative of
withdrawn maladjustment. Nevertheless, the manifest content of the items indicative of maladjustment usually indicated clearly whether the item described aggressive or
withdrawn behavior.

Ullmann's list provided us with a large number of
statements indicative of good adjustment and of withdrawn
maladjustment, as well as nondiscriminative items, and a
small number of items indicative of aggressive maladjustment. Altogether, about forty-five of our ninety statements were taken from Ullmann's list, and were grouped so
that statements of similar rater-preference value were together in a given item. While we do not know the rater-
preference or discriminative values of the items that
we added, experience with Ullmann's list probably made us
fairly skilful in devising such new items.

Scoring and statistical treatment.--After the ratings
for each child had been made, the total number of statements selected as most like for each of the three dimensions and as least like for each of these dimensions was
determined. Thus, there were obtained six "basic" scores:
most like leadership, aggressive maladjustment, and withdrawn maladjustment, and "least like each of these characteristics. The child's final score for each of the three
characteristics was then computed by combining the most
like quantity for the characteristic in question with the
two least like quantities for the other two characteristics. The most like quantity was weighted by multiplying
it by two. A child's score for leadership, for example,
was composed of his "basic" score on most like leadership
multiplied by two, plus his basic scores for least like
withdrawn maladjustment and aggressive maladjustment. In
addition to the final scores for each of these three characteristics, the basic scores were combined in two other ways.
The basic most like leadership and aggressive maladjustment scores and the 'least like withdrawn maladjustment
score were added to constitute a score which, perhaps un-
fortunately, came to be referred to as "masculinity." The
basic scores for most like withdrawn and aggressive maladjustment and least like leadership were added to constitute a maladjustment score without reference to the aggressive or withdrawn directions. These procedures are
summarized in Table 2.

Five scores, therefore, were obtained from the Behavior Description Chart: leadership, withdrawn maladjustment,
aggressive maladjustment, masculinity, and maladjustment.
A distribution of the scores for each of these traits was
made for the entire experimental group, and each score was
subsequently converted to a percentile rank.

Results.--In general, the results of the Behavior Description Chart appear to be consistent with expectations.
Table 3 gives means and standard deviations for each sex
on each of four scores (not including masculinity) obtained
from the instrument.

TABLE 2

Composition of Scores from Behavior
Description Chart

Basic Scores

Most Like:

```
Total leadership              = LE
Total withdrawn maladjustment = WI
Total aggressive maladjustment = AG
```

Least Like:

```
Total leadership              = le
Total withdrawn maladjustment = wi
Total aggressive maladjustment = ag
```

Final Scores

```
Leadership                = 2LE + wi + ag
Withdrawn maladjustment   = 2WI + le + ag
Aggressive maladjustment  = 2AG + le + wi
"Masculinity"             = LE + AG + wi
Maladjustment             = WI + AG + le
```

TABLE 3

Average Scores of Boys and Girls on
Behavior Description Chart

Quality	Boys (N = 187)		Girls (N = 215)	
	Mean	Standard Deviation	Mean	Standard Deviation
Leadership	21.3	13.0	28.1	14.8
Withdrawn maladjustment .	15.8	9.5	15.9	8.3
Aggressive maladjustment .	11.9	8.8	7.4	6.0
Maladjustment . .	10.5	7.9	4.8	5.7

It is characteristic of the method of scoring that most children are given scores close to zero, since most children would be rated by the judges as <u>most like</u> many of the neutral or nondiscriminating items. There are no negative scores. Because of these factors, the standard deviation is somewhat misleading, and correlation coefficients computed from these distributions should be interpreted with caution. The advantage of this system of scoring is that it identifies the deviate children clearly--the children with high scores on leadership and aggressive and withdrawn maladjustment. Certain other advantages, however, would have been gained by a simple scoring procedure which gave a child 1 for each "discriminating" statement on which he was rated as <u>most like</u>, -1 for each "discriminating" statement on which he was rated as <u>least like</u>, and 0 for each "nondiscriminating" statement on which he was rated as either <u>most like</u> or <u>least like</u>. Thus, the child would receive three scores on leadership, aggressive maladjustment, and withdrawn maladjustment, which might range from +18 to -18, and the group average would be in the neighborhood of zero. We expect to experiment further with both scoring methods.

It was probably to be expected, on the basis of the particular items used, that girls of this age would score higher on leadership and that boys would score higher on aggressive maladjustment. Because of the noticeable sex difference in the latter case and because of sex difference in the mode of expression of aggressive maladjustment, percentile scores were computed on the basis of separate sex distributions.

<u>Reliability of the instrument</u>.--Two aspects of the reliability of this instrument need to be considered. In the first place, we need to know with what consistency two or more judges can compare an individual with the rest of the group in respect to the desired characteristics. The extent of this consistency can be seen in the correlations of the scores of 73 girls for whom the Behavior Description Chart was filled out both by their teacher and by the leader of their Girl Scout troop. Since the Scout Leader sees the girls in situations quite different from that in which the teacher sees them, this is a rather severe test of re-

liability. Actually, the product-moment correlation coefficients of the scores for the several pairs of teacher and Scout Leaders varied from -.12 to .96 as shown in Table 4. The scores on withdrawn maladjustment are least reliable, according to this test, while those on aggressive maladjustment are most reliable. One teacher-Scout Leader pair (C in the table) shows practically no agreement. In every group of girls the teacher and Scout Leader disagreed widely on one or two girls. While the number of girls rated by a given pair of judges did not exceed sixteen and consequently the probable errors of the correlation coefficients are quite high, the averages of the correlation coefficients give some notion of what we might expect if our judges had rated larger numbers of girls. In general, the correlations are so low that it would seem essential to average the scores from at least two judges in order to arrive at a reasonably reliable result.

It should be noted that this group of girls made a rather poor sample for a test of reliability, not only because it represents only one sex, but also because it included few maladjusted girls. The correlations in Table 4 certainly underestimate the reliability of the instrument, but they also show clearly the need for ratings from at least two adults, one of whom should not be a teacher. We are inclined to believe that much of the difference between the two groups of raters was due to the fact that they saw the girls in different situations and that the girls actually behaved differently in these different situations.

In addition to this correlational comparison, we need to know the extent to which scores from different judges might vary in absolute degree because of differences in severity or leniency. Some indication of this may be seen in Table 5, although, again, a poor sample is used. If the means of the ratings from the six teacher-Scout Leader pairs are nearly equal, we may infer that the instrument does overcome differences in severity and leniency between the pairs of judges. The means are fairly close together for the members of each pair except Pair A, where the teacher is far more lenient than the Scout Leader.

From these reliability studies we have concluded that we must be very cautious in the interpretations we make on

TABLE 4

Coefficients of Correlation between Teacher
Ratings and Girl Scout Leader Ratings
on Behavior Description Chart

Sample	Number of Girls Rated	Leader-ship	With-drawn Malad-justment	Aggres-sive Malad-justment	General Malad-justment
A . .	8	.63	.32	.81	.81
B . .	16	.32	.36	.60	.25
C . .	14	.44	-.12	.18	.13
D . .	12	.25	.42	.19	.64
E . .	13	.62	.51	.96	.38
F . .	10	.75	.59	.31	.73
Average	..	.50	.35	.51	.49

TABLE 5

Comparison of Means of Teacher (T) and Girl Scout
Leader (SL) Ratings on Behavior Description Chart

Sample	Number of Girls Rated	Leadership		Withdrawn Maladjustment		Aggressive Maladjustment		General Maladjustment	
		Teacher	Scout Leader	Teacher	Scout Leader	Teacher	Scout Leader	Teacher	Scout Leader
A . .	8	37.0	17.6	15.8	18.6	11.0	15.3	7.5	12.1
B . .	16	23.6	21.4	17.9	12.7	8.7	12.6	7.4	6.2
C . .	14	27.5	26.8	16.5	18.5	6.0	8.1	4.4	6.6
D . .	12	33.6	32.7	12.8	13.8	6.1	9.9	2.2	4.2
E . .	13	31.6	29.6	11.2	12.6	6.1	7.0	1.2	2.6
F . .	10	28.2	23.7	18.2	15.5	6.0	7.6	6.3	5.3
Mean	73	29.5	25.7	15.4	15.0	7.2	9.9	4.7	5.8

the basis of scores from only one use of the Behavior Description Chart by one judge. We must get ratings from
more than one judge, and from non-teachers as well as
teachers.

The Guess-Who Test

Children's evaluation of their peers in regard to maladjustment and social leadership was made possible through
the administration of a Guess-Who test entitled "Who Are
They?" Nineteen items in all were included: five items indicative of social leadership, five of aggressive maladjustment, five of withdrawn maladjustment, one positive and one
negative friendship item, and two items intended to help select children who possessed a great deal of what might be
called "practical intelligence." Inspection of results indicated that the latter two items were largely unsuccessful.

The test was administered to the children in their
classrooms. Each child was given a sheet of the test items
and another sheet on which were listed the names of all the
children in the school in the subject's grade level. The
children were instructed to read the descriptive items and
to respond by putting the letter designation of the item before the names of all children to whom the description applied. Children were instructed not to sign their names to
their paper nor to put any letters next to their own name.
(The Guess-Who Test, entitled "Who Are They?" appears in
Appendix H.)

The items of this instrument were mostly taken from
similar instruments used in the Moral Character Study (1),
and they paralleled in content the items of the Behavior
Description Chart. Since the procedure was standard, and
most of the items had been used successfully previously,
no study was made of the reliability of this instrument.

Scoring and statistical treatment.--For each child,
the total number of mentions for each of the characteristics was determined. Because of the differences in the
number of children in the classrooms and the differences in
the number of classrooms of the subjects' grade within the
school, these totals could obviously not be used, without
modification, as indications of maladjustment and leadership. Two alternative methods of scoring were therefore

considered: (1) to use the per cent of the subject's total
mentions for leadership and for one or the other form of
maladjustment for his score in that category, and (2) to attempt to give some weight to the frequency of mention per se
by using some means to equate the differences mentioned
above. The second alternative was decided upon. The total
number of mentions for a given characteristic, then, was divided in each case by the mean total number of responses
which children in the subject's classroom received for leadership, withdrawn maladjustment, and aggressive maladjustment combined. This gave scores for the three characteristics. By this method, a child who was mentioned very seldom
would get a low score, even though his mentions were all favorable or all unfavorable.

In addition, a score for friendship was computed on the
basis of mentions on positive and negative friendship items.
Three types of friendship relations were given weight in the
friendship score: being desired as a friend, being ignored
by one's peers in regard to friendship, and being rejected
or not wanted as a friend. In the computing of the friendship score, peer judgments were used only in those cases in
which the child had indicated some acquaintance with the
subject by a mention for some item on the Guess-Who Test.
Weights were arbitrarily assigned in computing the friendship score as follows: two for a positive mention for friendship, minus one for no mention in regard to friendship, and
minus two for rejection as a friend. The total of these was
then divided by the total number of children in the subject's school grade who had expressed acquaintance through
mentions on one or more items of the test. To the result-
ing number was added 200 in order to avoid negative scores.

All four scores (on leadership, withdrawn maladjustment,
aggressive maladjustment, and friendship) were then converted to percentile ranks.

Results.--Means and standard deviations of each sex for
each of the four scores are given in Table 6. On this instrument boys rated somewhat higher than girls on leadership
as well as on aggressive maladjustment. Again, because of
sex differences in aggressive maladjustment, percentile
ranks were assigned on the basis of separate sex distributions.

TABLE 6

Average Scores for Boys and Girls in Guess-Who Test

Quality	Boys (N = 176)		Girls (N = 224)	
	Mean	Standard Deviation	Mean	Standard Deviation
Leadership	66.1	31.8	62.5	39.2
Withdrawn maladjustment	20.0	12.8	22.4	13.7
Aggressive maladjustment	24.9	24.8	14.2	13.9
Friendship	197.7	58.6	203.5	55.2

Selection of Leaders and Maladjusted Children

Nine lists were drawn up for maladjustment, on which were ranked the children who were highest with respect to the following:

Behavior Description Chart score for --

1. Withdrawn maladjustment
2. Aggressive maladjustment
3. "General" maladjustment

Guess-Who score for--

4. Withdrawn maladjustment
5. Aggressive maladjustment
6. "General" maladjustment (mean of the percentile ranks for withdrawn maladjustment and aggressive maladjustment)

Mean of percentile ranks on Behavior Description Chart and Guess-Who for--

7. Withdrawn maladjustment
8. Aggressive maladjustment
9. "General" maladjustment

In assigning names of children to the case loads of counselor teams, equal numbers of names were drawn from each of these lists. Since there was, of course, a great deal of overlapping of names on the lists, the process of selecting a specific number of children for assignment was carried out by going to whatever depth on the lists was necessary to produce names of the required number of individuals.

For leadership a similar plan was followed. Since both instruments resulted in substantially more girls than

boys at the high end of the distribution, it seemed wise to
have a separate list for boys and girls and to draw equally
from these. Consequently, the following lists were drawn
up, three lists of boys and three lists of girls: (1) Behavior Description Chart score, (2) Guess-Who score, and
(3) mean of the percentile rank for Scores 1 and 2. For
each sex, names were drawn equally from these lists until
the desired number of individuals was reached.

Relations Between Scores on the Two Instruments

In order to explore some of the relations between
scores for leadership and maladjustment, as well as between
scores from the two instruments, the product-moment correlation coefficients shown in Table 7 were computed. In general, the correlations are about what would be expected, and
they justify confidence in the usefulness of the instruments.

From this table it will be seen that socioeconomic status is more highly related to leadership among girls than
among boys. (A high socioeconomic index means low socioeconomic status.)

The table throws some light on the question of the
distinction between aggressive and withdrawn maladjustment.
Can they be clearly distinguished in their early manifesta-
tions? Are they clearly distinguished by our instruments?

On the Behavior Description Chart there are small negative correlations between scores on aggressive and withdrawn maladjustment. For the girls this correlation is neg-
ligibly different from zero. These coefficients indicate
either no association or a slight negative association between the two forms of maladjustment, but not the high negative relation that exists, for example, between leadership
and either form of maladjustment. It is to be noted from
Table 7, however, that the withdrawn maladjustment and aggressive maladjustment scores on the Behavior Description
Chart have a small positive correlation "built in" them,
because these scores each include the "least-like" score
for leadership.

The Guess-Who instrument does not distinguish so clearly between withdrawn and aggressive maladjustment, for there
are small positive correlations between the two. This may
be due to the relative inability of children at this age to
observe the distinctions that we are trying to make between

TABLE 7

Product-Moment Correlation Coefficients between Scores on Guess-Who Test and Behavior Description Chart for 176 Fourth-Grade Boys (above Diagonal Line) and for 215 Fourth-Grade Girls (below Diagonal Line)

	Socioeconomic Status	Guess-Who Test				Behavior Description Chart				
		Leadership	Withdrawn Maladjustment	Aggressive Maladjustment	Friendship	Leadership	Withdrawn Maladjustment	Aggressive Maladjustment	Masculinity	General Maladjustment
Socioeconomic Status		-.20	.10	.22	.00	-.27	.04	.29	-.03	.25
Guess-Who Test:										
Leadership	-.42		-.43	-.28	.44	.57	.28			
Withdrawn maladjustment	.18	-.34		.29	-.26					
Aggressive maladjustment	.15	-.20	.21		-.43			.61		
Friendship	-.37	-.62	-.45	.23						
Behavior Description Chart:										
Leadership	-.42	.66					.53	-.52		-.86
Withdrawn maladjustment	.18		.40			-.63		.21		.61
Aggressive maladjustment	.23			.52		-.43				.61
Masculinity	.31						-.04			
General maladjustment	-.33					-.81	.73	.61		

the beginnings of aggressive and withdrawn maladjustment,
or it may be due to some characteristic of the Guess-Who
Test items.

As a practical result of the use of these instruments,
we are including in the group for further study and help
some children who seem to be potentially maladjusted, although we do not know whether this maladjustment can be
classified as aggressive or withdrawn.

The group of potential leaders is distinguished clearly from the potentially maladjusted group. Some of the
leaders are also in the group selected for intellectual talent, as is shown in chapter 6. The coefficient of correlation of intelligence quotient with leadership (in the Guess-
Who Test) is .38 for boys and .41 for girls.

Bibliography

1. Havighurst, Robert J., and Taba, Hilda. Adolescent Character and Personality, chap. xix. New York: John Wiley
   & Sons, 1949.

2. Hewitt, Lester Eugene, and Jenkins, Richard L., M.D.
   Fundamental Patterns of Maladjustment. Springfield,
   Illinois: State of Illinois, 1946.

3. Jenkins, Richard L., M.D., and Glickman, Sylvia. "Common
   Syndromes in Child Psychiatry," American Journal of Orthopsychiatry, XVI (April, 1946), 244-61.

4. Jenkins, Richard L., M.D., and Hewitt, Lester Eugene.
   "Types of Personality Structure Encountered in Child
   Guidance Clinics," American Journal of Orthopsychiatry,
   XIV (1944), 84-94.

5. Sisson, E. Donald. "Forced Choice: The New Army Rating,"
   Personnel Psychology, I (1948), 365-81.

6. Ullmann, Charles A. The Identification of Maladjusted
   School Children. Public Health Monograph No. 7. Public
   Health Service Publication No. 211. Washington: Govern-
   ment Printing Office, 1952.

CHAPTER 5

DISCOVERY OF TALENT IN THE ARTS

To discover talent in the field of the fine arts it is necessary first to decide what particular areas are to be considered. We decided to look for potential talent in four areas: graphic arts, music, writing, and drama. In these fields the procedures for discovering gifted children are less fully developed than they are for discovering children with intellectual ability. Objective tests for discovering artistic ability are still inadequate and yield inconclusive results.

For this reason we developed a method whereby the community assisted in the screening procedure. First, artistic productions were obtained from children in the experimental and the control groups. Second, four committees composed, respectively, of practicing artists, writers, musicians, dramatists, and other persons in the community who were interested in these arts were organized for the specific purpose of evaluating the merits of the artistic productions of the children. The children producing the best work, as judged by the committees, were selected for further study and help.

Community residents interested in music, art, writing, and drama were invited to an organizational meeting in the winter of 1952. The work of the project was described to the group by the consultant staff, and the problems of identifying talent were discussed. The four working committees were established at this meeting. During the following year (1952-53) all but the dramatics committee worked on the initial problem of identifying children with talents in the respective areas.

Committees such as these can probably be organized in almost any community, and offer a possible procedure for selecting talented children in fields in which objective tests have been unsatisfactory.

Work of the Art Committee

Two characteristics of the work of this committee were notable. First, the committee worked as a group in judging the drawings. Second, they showed a great amount of concern for the children behind the drawings; members expressed the sentiment that they did not want to overlook any child because of careless rating.

This desire to work together and the concern for children arose partly from the extreme importance of the subjective decisions of the judges, which resulted from the lack of objective procedure on which the committee could rely. The committee was united by its feeling of inadequacy, and it experimented with a number of rating procedures, working slowly and carefully.

The drawing assignments.--A drawing test was administered by the teachers in the fourth and the sixth grades of the public schools in the spring of 1952. The test consisted of four drawing assignments, which were given in the following order: (1) Draw-a-Man Test (1), (2) a drawing of the schoolroom, (3) a scenic picture, and (4) a drawing of a favorite subject. The following directions were given to the teachers:

1. The Draw-a-Man Assignment

This needs to be given under standard conditions for all children since the results can be used to assess the developmental level of children as well as their artistic ability. Therefore the following instructions need to be followed closely.

Each child should be provided with a pencil and a sheet of drawing paper. Crayons should not be used. Before beginning, see that all books and pictures are put away, so that there will be no opportunity for copying. The following instructions are then given to the children:

"On these papers I want you to make a picture of a person. Make the very best picture that you can. Make a picture of the whole person. Take your time and work very carefully. I want to see whether the boys and girls in (school's name) school can do as well as those in other schools. Try very hard and see what good pictures you can make."

As the drawings are being made, the examiner should stroll about the room to see that instructions are being followed, and encourage, by means of a little judicious praise, anyone who seems to need it. In doing this, it is best to avoid calling attention to the work of any individual child; rather, let the comments be of a general nature, such as, "These drawings are fine; you boys and girls are doing very well," etc. Never make adverse comments or criticism, and under no circumstances should a child's attention be called to any errors or omissions in his work, however gross they may be. Answer all questions by saying, "Do it whatever way you think is best."

The importance of avoiding every kind of suggestion cannot be overemphasized. Not only must the examiner himself refrain from all remarks which could influence the nature of the drawings (the only exception to this rule is noted in a following paragraph), but he must see to it that no suggestions come from the children. They should not be permitted to hold up their drawings for admiration or comment in such a way that other children may see them, or to make audible remarks about their work. If permitted to do so, little children are very likely to accompany their performance by a running fire of description, such as, "I'm giving my man a soldier hat," "Mine's going to have a big, long pipe," etc. While it is true that these comments are most likely to have to do with appurtenances which do not affect the score, there is danger that a child who attempts to carry out such suggestions may thereby have his attention so distracted from his original concept as to cause him to forget some of the essential parts of his drawing in his interest in this new, and probably unimportant, detail.

The examiner must not, however, lose sight of this fact: It is essential for the validity of the test that each child make the best effort of which he is capable. To secure such effort, a cheerful, sympathetic attitude must be adopted throughout. The child who is bursting with eagerness to tell about his drawing must be suppressed, it is true, but never in such a way as to dampen his enthusiasm. A firm but good-natured, "No one must tell about his picture now. Wait until everybody has finished," will usually dispose of such cases without affecting the general interest or disturbing the rapport which should exist between examiner and children.

There is no time limit for the test, but children rarely take more than five or ten minutes. If one or two children are slower than the rest, it is best to collect papers from those who have finished, and allow them to go on with their regular work while the slower workers are finishing.

The following special circumstances should be noted: (1) It sometimes happens that through erasure or other accident a child may spoil his drawing. In such cases he should always be given a fresh sheet and be allowed to try again. All such instances should be noted on the back of the sheet. (2) In grades above the second, it will occasionally be found that a child has drawn a bust picture only. When it is evident that this has been the intention, a fresh paper should be given and the child told to "make the whole man." Both papers should be preserved for comparison.

2. Schoolroom Drawing

The following instructions are read to the children:

"Look around at your classroom. Notice everything you can about it. Draw a picture of the room showing how it looks to you as you enter the doorway. If you wish, you may look at the room from the doorway. Remember, you are to make a picture showing how the schoolroom looks to you without the other children or teacher in it. Use only a pencil to make the best drawing you can. Now begin. . . . When you are finished write your name on the back."

3. Scenic Picture

This picture must be done in water colors or crayons, not pencil (although pencil may be used for preliminary sketch). Have crayons and water colors ready. The following instructions are read to the children.

"On the page in front of you make a picture of some scene you would like to see next summer. Shut your eyes for just a moment. Try to imagine some landscape or view you would very much like to see on your next summer vacation. Now open your eyes and draw it. Use either crayons or water colors to make your picture. Make as good a picture as you can. . . . When you are finished write your name on the back."

If anyone asks if he may draw something he has seen on past vacations, he is to be permitted to do so.

4. Favorite-Subject Assignment

The following instructions are read to the children:

"Make a drawing of whatever you like best to draw. It can be a picture of anything at all, but it must be in color. Use either water colors or crayons. Make this a picture of whatever you like best to draw. . . . When you are finished write your name on the back."

Judging the pictures.--The Art Committee was asked to select the best drawings in each of the four assignments at each grade level. The committee developed a four-step method, each step reducing the number of pictures to be given further study.

> 1. Elimination of all pictures which showed no promise whatever.
>
> 2. Rating the remainder on a three-point scale. Those rated lowest were discarded. Those getting a rating of 1 or 2 were retained for further study.
>
> 3. Rating the remaining pictures on the basis of objective criteria, giving a numerical score to each picture. These scores provided a quantitative basis for ranking the pictures in order of merit.
>
> 4. Subjective confirmation of objective rating.

Table 8 shows the number of pictures that were retained in each step of the judging procedure for the experimental group. There were 450 pictures from each assignment.

The first step was a rough screening to cull out the obviously poor drawings. The pictures were held up one at

a time under an adequate light, and the committee passed
judgment on each picture. The pictures were put into two
groups labeled "good" and "no merit." Judging was very
lenient; if only one person in the group thought a picture
was good, it was retained.

TABLE 8

Drawings Retained at Each Step in Screening
450 Drawings from Each of Four Assignments

Step	Assignment 1		Assignment 2		Assignment 3		Assignment 4	
	Number	Per Cent	Number	Per Cent	Number	Per Cent	Number	Per Cent
1. .	87	19.0	55	12.0	115	25.0	104	23.0
2. .	44	9.6	21	4.6	74	16.2	30	6.7
3-4 .	20	4.4	20	4.4	20	4.4	20	4.4

It is interesting to see how the distribution of drawings selected in the first step compares with a distribution that might be expected if the drawings had been selected by chance, or if drawings had been selected at random on
the assumption that all the children had the same drawing
ability, as judged by the committee. The numbers of children
who would have had four, three, two, and one drawings selected respectively, if ninety drawings were selected by
chance from each assignment, may be compared with the observed numbers:

Chance	0.7	12	69	184
Observed	11	19	49	162

Thus, eleven children actually had all four of their
drawings selected, whereas by chance less than one child
would have had all four of his drawings selected. Nineteen
children had three of their drawings selected, against a
chance expectation of twelve.

In the second step the pictures were again judged one
at a time and given a rating of 1, 2, or 3. Pictures rated
3 were eliminated. The rating was more critical this time,
but not necessarily more objective. The committee discussed the pictures and gave more careful consideration to
them than in the previous step. In this step the name of
the child was masked, and the pictures were given a code
number.

In the third step the pictures were rated objectively, again by the entire committee. The pictures were rated on the basis of the following nine criteria. These criteria were based, to a large extent, on the studies made of children's drawings at the Cleveland Museum of Art (2). A five-point scale was set up for each criterion, and a total score for each drawing was obtained by summing the ratings it received on the criteria. Instructions for using the criteria were provided and are shown in Appendix D. The numbers 1-5 under each criterion are the five points on the scale used to rate the drawings.

I. Representational ability

    1. Primitive schema
    2. Schema
    3. Mixed
    4. True to appearance
    5. Perspective

II. Line technique

    1. Hesitating, timid, ragged
    2. Clumsy, fine
    3. Decisive, firm
    4. Bold
    5. Discriminating, subtle, and bold

III. Area technique

    1. Ragged, scratchy
    2. Smooth, uniform
    3. Bold, saturated, vigorous
    4. Graded and blended
    5. Textured, molded

IV. Flexibility of objects

    1. Objects stiff, wooden
    3. Some stiff, some flexible
    5. Objects fit, freedom, lifelike

V. Compositional unity

    1. Organization not attempted, random
    2. Linear, ground line used
    3. Objects related in space, and decorative
       pattern
   4-5. Only one object represented, but well
       proportioned
   4-5. Successful, unusual organization

VI. Color

    1. Indiscriminate, unrealistic, unpleasant
       pattern
    3. Good color sense and value, bright, clear
    5. Outstanding contrasts gained

VII. Artistic movement--path of vision

    1. No path of vision, eye leaves picture
    3. Partly successful path of vision, some
       major elements of picture left out
    5. Eye stays in picture, major parts of
       picture included in path

VIII. Creative liberty

    1. Bizarre, rejected assignment
    3. Mechanically bound by assignment, con-
       ventional, stereotyped
    5. Self-expressive, inventive

IX. Communicativeness

    1. Dull
    3. Predominantly dull, some show of vitality
    5. Fresh, eager, insightful

The committee considered the last two criteria to be among the most important to judge and yet the most diffi- cult. It was felt that the last two criteria should rate the success with which the artist captured a scene, his feelings about the scene, and his communication of it to the audience.

On the pictures of the first assignment (Draw-a-Man) the committee used only Criteria I, II, IV, V, and VIII and IX in combination. A note of explanation is in order here. This assignment was the last to be scored on an objective basis. As a result of its experience with the score sheet, the committee felt that Criteria VIII and IX were so much alike that they should be combined. Criteria dealing with color, artistic movement, or with area technique were not appropriate to this assignment. Compositional unity was interpreted as placement of the object in this assignment rather than as relationship of objects to another, since there was only one object in the picture. The highest score that a Draw-a-Man picture could receive was 25.

On the second assignment (picture of the schoolroom), Criteria III and V were not applicable since they dealt with treatment of area and use of color. The highest score one of these pictures could receive was 35.

All the criteria were applicable to the pictures of the last two assignments since these were in color. The highest possible score for each of these two was 45.

A refinement was introduced in the third step of the judging procedure. The pictures were judged in groups rather than singly, as in the first two steps. From fif-

teen to twenty pictures were placed on the wall at one time,
and then all the pictures were rated on one criterion at a
time. This made possible a more analytical comparison between pictures rather than global judgments.

The final step was meant to be a subjective checking
process on the objective method of Step 3. Some committee
members had expressed doubts as to the validity of the objective method. Events showed these doubters to be correct,
since the ranks of the pictures according to merit were
changed in several instances from the rank orders of the
objective ratings. Evidently, the objective procedure is
not yet a completely adequate procedure.

In the final step the committee ranked the twenty best
pictures from each assignment in order of merit. This total of eighty pictures was the committee's final judgment
on the best work of the children.

At this point the work of judging the pictures was completed. The consultant staff did the technical work of selecting a number of children from among those who produced
the eighty best pictures.

Selecting the children.--Two criteria were used in
trying to find a formula by which to select the best per-
formers. One was excellence of work, and the second was
consistency of performance.

Excellence of drawing was first studied by taking the
best twenty pictures, the top five drawings in each of the
four assignments. Twenty different children produced these
twenty drawings. It is clear that at this high level none
of the children was consistent. Thirty-four children contributed the forty best pictures. Fifty-nine children contributed the eighty best. As the standard of excellence
was lowered, the consistency of performance increased.

A second method of determining the excellence of a
child's performance was to find the average rank given to
his pictures which had been placed among the best twenty
pictures in each assignment. Those who received an average
rank from 1 through 7 were rated high; from 8 through 14,
medium; from 15 through 20, low. Fifteen children received
a high rating; 29, medium; 15, low.

Consistency of drawing performance was measured by
counting the number of drawings each child placed among the

top twenty in the four assignments. Among the fifty-nine
children contributing the best eighty pictures, three children placed three drawings; fifteen placed two drawings;
and forty-one placed one drawing. Table 9 summarizes the
results of the process of selection based on excellence and
consistency. Asterisks indicate the children who produced
the five best drawings in the four assignments.

The conclusion was reached that the best method of selection was to choose the twenty children who produced the
twenty best drawings (five from each assignment). This number included all those who produced three pictures among
the eighty best, half of those who produced two, and about
a quarter of those who produced one. Ten other children
will be watched closely, namely, the seven who produced two
selected drawings that were ranked medium but not among the
twenty best, and the three who produced one drawing which
ranked high but not among the twenty best.

TABLE 9

Distribution of 59 Children According to Number of
Drawings Placed among the Top 80 in Four Assignments
and According to Average Rank of Pictures

Average Rank of Pictures	Number of Children Placing--			
	Three Drawings	Two Drawings	One Drawing	Total
High	1*	2*	9* 3	15
Medium	2*	6* 7	14	29
Low	0	0	15	15
Total	3	15	41	59

*Indicates children who produced the five best draw-
ings in the four assignments.

The Art Committee.--The committee met on an average of
twice a month for a period of eight months. The committee
was composed of ten members having a variety of interests,
amount of training, and aptitude in art. One was a produc-
tive painter who has private classes of children and adults;

another was an art historian; a third, a commercial artist;
two were teachers of art in the public schools; one was a
former art teacher; three painted as a hobby; and one person was interested in the general field of aesthetics. An
average of five members was present at every meeting. The
staff consultant was present at every meeting and kept a
record of the ratings and procedures.

It was clear from the beginning that two schools of
thought were represented on the committee: the "realistic"
school and the modern, "impressionistic" school. Representatives from each were inclined to favor the pictures which
exhibited their favorite style. However, the issue in rating the pictures was not drawn between realism and impres-
sionism but rather between excellence and mediocrity. Only
in the case of the first objective criterion, representational ability, was realism given priority. On the other
criteria, realistic pictures and impressionistic pictures
were thought to have equal chances of being scored high.

The opinion is sometimes expressed that training in
aesthetics and art criticism is necessary in order to do
the kind of judging required by this project. Such training was probably not necessary in this case since the task
was not one of rating, in an absolute sense, the aesthetic
merits of an isolated picture, but rather one of comparing
a number of pictures and ranking them in order of aesthetic
merit. Furthermore, the task of rejecting three-fourths of
the pictures as lacking merit and of selecting the best
five per cent was not extremely difficult. The difficulty
lay in judging the merits of the 20 per cent of the pictures in between.

A further note on the process of the committee is in
order. A certain amount of self-training by the committee
was necessary. In the first two steps, however, very little of this occurred. But in the third step it became necessary for the members to train themselves to be objective and
analytic, since it was impossible to express only a global
reaction of favor to, or rejection of, a picture. The members were required to dissociate themselves from their general emotional reaction to the picture and to analyze it in
terms of the objective criteria. This process was helpful
in preventing the committee, made up of representatives of

different schools of thought, from becoming deadlocked over preferences or dislikes. Soon after the objective process of rating was begun, such remarks as the following could be heard: "That picture leaves me cold, but I must admit the line technique is good." This kind of learning probably took place most readily in the group setting since the committee members forced one another to be objective.

A second learning took place when the committee was asked to rate the pictures on a five-point scale. The members could readily rate a picture qualitatively, as "high" or "low" on a given criterion, but when they were asked to rate it quantitatively, they were often unprepared to commit themselves. One of the tasks of the consultant was to remind the committee to rate the pictures quantitatively.

Work of the Writing Committee

The first task was to devise a series of assignments which would elicit creative writing from the children. Several assignments were tried out with children not in the project and were rejected before the following were chosen: (1) "The Most Exciting Event" (uncompleted story), (2) "The Person I Would Like To Be Like," (3) Letter to Grandmother, (4) Jumbled Words test, and (5) modified thematic apperception test. The instructions for these tests follow.

1. The Most Exciting Event (uncompleted story)

The teacher will read the following instructions:

"Today we are going to hear part of a story and then complete it. The story goes like this":

The Storybook Man was old. He was as old as the first story that was ever told. He carried a big, heavy basket strapped to his back, and he traveled everywhere.

The basket was full of books. There were big books and little books, funny stories and sad stories. There were stories about everything you could possibly think of.

The Storybook Man was happy because children all over the world loved his books. Everywhere he went, children came running out to see what books he had. Sometimes they wanted new books. At other times they wanted old ones, stories that had been read many, many times before.

One day, for the first time in his life, the Storybook Man was not happy. For that day the children wanted a new book, newer than any he had.

"We want a book that is newer than new," they said. "We want a book that nobody has ever read."

The Storybook Man reached down, down, far into his basket. Soon you could see nothing of him but his heels and one hand coming up from time to time with a book.

But each time the children called, "We've all read that one, Storybook Man. We want a book that nobody has ever read before."

Finally, the Storybook Man pulled himself up out of his basket. On his face was a wide smile. In his arms were some little thin books that the children had never seen before. There were no pictures on the covers. There were no names on the books.

The Storybook Man handed one of the books to each child. "Here is a book so new that nobody has ever read it. It is so new that it hasn't even been written."

"It must be about you, Storybook Man" said the children.

"No, it is about you. Nobody can tell a story about you as well as you can," answered the Storybook Man. "Just write your name on the first line. The rest will be easy."

The Storybook Man gave each child a pencil. Each child wrote his name, and then went on writing. The Storybook Man watched and smiled to hear the scratching pencils. At last the children stopped writing.

"Now," said the Storybook Man, "Listen!" He opened one of the little thin books and began to read. He read one story, and the children wanted another. He read two, and they wanted three. All the stories were about boys and girls and the exciting things they had done. Bill made up an adventure story about himself. Mary wrote a funny story about herself. Jim told of things he would like to do some day.

"Now imagine that you were one of the children there. Take your paper and pencil and write a story about yourself or an imaginary person--'a story so new it hasn't even been written.' It can be true or imaginary as you wish. Just write your name on the first line. The rest will be easy."

2. The Person I Would Like To Be Like

The teacher will read the following directions:

"Write a description of the person whom you would most like to be like when you grow up. Write at least a half-page about this person. This person may be a real person, or a make-believe person, a man or woman. He or she may be a combination of several people. Tell something about this person's age, character, appearance, the kind of work he does, his favorite recreation or pastime. Tell everything you can about why you would like to be like this person. If he is a real person, say so. You need not give his real name if you do not want to."

3. Letter to Grandmother

The teacher will read the following directions:

"Today we will have a chance to write a letter. Let's all pretend that we have a grandmother (or aunt) who lives on a farm and that we are going to tell her what we did over the week end. Let's say that grandmother always likes to hear from us and that she loves to know what we are doing. Your letter should not be much more than a page long. Just start the letter 'Dear Grandma.'"

4. Jumbled Words Test

The teacher will list the following words on the blackboard. She will then give the following instructions:

"On the blackboard I have listed ten word-pictures. I would like to have you write a story using at least four of them. Choose any four or more from the list and make up a story from them. You may write as much as you wish."

The words to be listed are:

1. Slippery sidewalks
2. Underground caverns
3. Bicycle with broken spoke
4. Sharp knife
5. Wooden raft
6. Magic pebble
7. Cozy fireside
8. Invisible castle
9. Drizzly rain
10. Crimson sunset

5. Thematic Apperception Test

The fifth test has not been completed at the time of this writing. A modified thematic apperception test is being considered, which might be scored for personality factors as well as for writing ability. Similarly, the essay on "The Person I Would Like To Be Like" may be used for the study of personality factors.

The Creative Writing Committee included eight persons, all of whom were actively engaged in writing, teaching of writing, or library work. One of them was the faculty sponsor of the high-school weekly newspaper; another, the sponsor of the junior high-school paper. Two were librarians, one of them at the high-school and the other at the children's department of the public library. One person was a script writer for a local radio broadcasting station; another, a free-lance writer and reporter. Also included were a college instructor of English and the supervisor of curriculum development and testing in the public schools.

Work of the Music Committee

The music committee was composed of nine members, all of whom were practicing musicians. The committee included

the conductor of the community symphony orchestra, another
member of the orchestra, four of the administrators and instructors in the music department of the public schools,
and three private teachers of music, both instrumental and
voice.

The music committee decided to follow a three-point
program. (1) They decided to collect information about the
children who rated superior, excellent, and very good on the
musical-aptitude test given as a regular part of the program in the public schools--the Tilson-Gretsch Music Aptitude Test, which was given to both the experimental and the
control groups. On the basis of this test, ten children in
the experimental group rated superior, thirty-four rated
excellent, and forty-three rated very good. The test consists of tests of pitch and intensity discrimination and of
tonal memory. In the case of the children with high ratings,
the committee planned to find out who were taking music lessons, who had discontinued such lessons, and who had never
shown any interest in lessons. (2) The committee will devise further methods of testing or discovering musical aptitude, if possible. (3) They decided to study personality
traits and interests which successful musicians displayed
in their childhood. The committee thought this might be a
useful approach to an alternative method of identifying
promising young musicians.

This program resulted from a feeling that present tests
of musical aptitude leave much to be desired. Interest and
motivation are not tested with these tests. Musicianship
was seen as being a more complex set of functions than is
tested with present aptitude tests. For these reasons, the
committee was reluctant to accept the results of the school
tests as sufficient, although it was thought that they
would be useful. A major task of this committee will be to
discover children with musical aptitude who do not now dis-
play any interest in music.

Bibliography

1. Goodenough, Florence. Measuring Intelligence by Means
   of Drawings. Yonkers-on-Hudson, New York: World Book
   Co., 1926.

2. Lark-Horowitz, Betty. "Children's Art Abilities: Studies at the Cleveland Museum of Art," Journal of Experimental Education, XI (December, 1942), 115-55.

CHAPTER 6

CHARACTERISTICS OF THE SELECTED CHILDREN

In order to throw some light on the nature of children who most strongly exhibit those characteristics of interest or concern to the Youth Development Program, an exploratory study was made comparing the selected groups. Further research of a more penetrating nature is being planned for this area, and the present investigation was limited to data already on hand and routinely collected for each child in the experimental and the control groups.

Procedure

Groups were formed of the twenty highest children in each of the following categories: (1) the consistently intellectually gifted, (2) the specialized intellectually gifted, (3) leaders, (4) the withdrawn maladjusted, (5) the aggressively maladjusted, and (6) the artistically gifted (as judged by drawing tests). The methods by which children were measured and selected for these characteristics have been described in preceding chapters.

These groups were compared on the basis of the standing of each group on nineteen measurements:

1. Index of Status Characteristics (socioeconomic statu
2. Primary Mental Abilities intelligence quotient (Elementary Form)
3. Draw-a-Man intelligence quotient
4. Davis-Eells Games (general intelligence)

From Primary Mental Abilities (for ages 11-17):

5. Verbal meaning
6. Space
7. Reasoning
8. Street Gestalt Completion test (C_1)
9. Concealed Figures test (C_2)

From Behavior Description Chart:

10. Leadership
11. Withdrawn maladjustment
12. Aggressive maladjustment
13. "Masculinity"
14. General maladjustment

From Who Are They Test:

15. Leadership
16. Withdrawn maladjustment
17. Aggressive maladjustment
18. Friendship
19. Four-drawing test (drawing ability)

The mean score for each group was computed for the first eighteen of these measurements. So that these groups might be compared on a common scale and might also be compared with the "average" child in the total experimental group, the group means for measurements 4 through 18 were expressed in the percentile rank equivalent of these values. Measurements 2 and 3 are in the form of intelligence quotients, and measurement 1 is an arbitrary value described in chapter 7. High scores on measurement 1 indicate low status, and vice versa.

Table 10 summarizes these data. As the reader will notice, none of the six groups is used in comparisons on the categories by means of which the group was selected, nor on closely related categories.

In regard to drawing ability, a crude comparison between the groups was made by placing each group on a 100-point scale. Fifty-nine children had been selected as having a noticeable degree of competence in drawing and had been ranked roughly in order of merit. Some of the children in whom we are primarily interested were in this group of fifty-nine and also in one of the selected groups aside from the group selected for drawing ability. The score, then, for each of the groups of selected children with whom we are primarily concerned was determined by the average ranking of its members within this group of fifty-nine children. The total scores for the five groups were then made to fit a 100-point scale.

Results

From this procedure we are able to get a rough picture of the "average" child in each of the selected groups in terms of certain available information. No attempt will be made to determine the statistical reliability of the differences between groups until we have more reliable measurements for use in the screening program.

TABLE 10

Comparison of Selected Groups on Nineteen Measurements

Measurement	Score for Group*					
	Consistently Intellectually Gifted	Specialized Intellectually Gifted	Leadership	Withdrawn Maladjustment	Aggressive Maladjustment	Talented in Drawing
Number of pupils in group:						
Boys	15	10	10	10	10	9
Girls	15	10	10	10	10	11
1. Index of Status Characteristics	41	57	50	55	62	52
2. I.Q. on Primary Mental Abilities	...	...	114	90	96	112
3. I.Q. on Draw-a-Man	...	...	108	94	97	117
4. Davis-Eells Games	...	...	70	36	57	70
From Primary Mental Abilities:						
5. Verbal meaning	...	...	65	41	47	72
6. Space	...	...	65	38	41	72
7. Reasoning	...	...	64	30	38	64
8. Street Gestalt Completion (C_1)	...	...	69	26	50	69
9. Concealed Figures test (C_2)	...	...	75	32	46	84
From Behavior Description Chart:						
10. Leadership	88	55	...	20	27	69
11. Withdrawn maladjustment	23	52	38	...	...	44
12. Aggressive maladjustment	58	59	46	...	...	59
13. Masculinity	92	55	87	17	78	74
14. General maladjustment	44	62	44	...	...	57
From Who Are They?						
15. Leadership	85	74	...	19	25	74
16. Withdrawn maladjustment	34	41	26	...	...	35
17. Aggressive maladjustment	60	62	45	...	...	67
18. Friendship	63	60	84	27	21	48
19. Four-drawing test	53	14	29	3	1	...

*Scores for measurements 4-18 are mean percentiles.

The consistently intellectually gifted child, as might
be expected, shows superiority in most of the categories on
which he was compared. His socioeconomic status is the
highest of the six groups; he is a leader to a greater extent than members of the four comparable groups; he appears
to be out-going and assertive within the area of sanction
of teacher and peers; he has many friends. Even in drawing he excels.

The specialized intellectually gifted child seems to
differ from the preceding group in degree rather than in
pattern. Socially and personally he does not appear to be
out of the ordinary. His most striking difference from
the consistent intellectually gifted child lies in his considerably lower socioeconomic status.

The leader group shows relatively high socioeconomic
status and a consistent superiority on all the intellectual
measures. In personality and social relations this group
is expectedly well off. Attractiveness as a friend is the
most outstanding of the characteristics measured. The
standing of this group in drawing may be debated, as might
that of the consistently intellectually gifted, since twenty-
four points of the total for each of these groups is scored
by two individuals who are members of both groups.

The withdrawn maladjusted children appear, on the basis
of this comparison, to be the dullest intellectually and the
most passive but to surpass the aggressive maladjusted children in a socioeconomic status. The latter children are
also well below the average of the total group in intellectual abilities, are the lowest status group, and the least
liked. Only about twelve or thirteen of the maladjusted
groups took the Verbal Meaning, Space, and Reasoning tests
of the Primary Mental Abilities, the Street Gestalt Completion test (C_1), and the Concealed Figures test (C_2). Probably those who did not take these tests would have had
scores lower than those who did because many children scoring low on the Primary Mental Abilities, Elementary Form,
were not given this battery of tests.

The artistically gifted show a surprising degree of
intellectual ability. The mean intelligence quotient on
the Draw-a-Man test probably indicates that the ability to
draw well helps the child to achieve a higher score on this

test. This group had the highest mean of comparable groups on the space factor and the second closure factor, both of which can be seen to bear some relationship to drawing ability. Their personality picture looks good in general, although they stand considerably lower than the other three gifted groups in relation to desirability as a friend.

It should be remembered, in considering the ratios of the sexes, that the numbers of boys and girls were arbitrarily made equal in the groups with drawing ability and with special intellectual talent, leadership, and aggressive maladjustment.

Since the degree of overlapping membership of these selected groups may have some bearing on the comparisons presented above, and since this seems to be a question of general interest, the numbers of overlapping cases are presented in Table 11. The consistently intellectually gifted group accounted for eight out of fourteen cases of overlapping. All but one of these were in relation to another area of giftedness.

TABLE 11

Overlapping in Selected Groups of Children

Group	Consistently Intellectually Gifted	Specialized Intellectually Gifted	Leaders	Withdrawn Maladjustment	Aggressive Maladjustment
Specialized intellectually gifted	. .	. .	. .	. .	. .
Leaders	4	1		. .	. .
Withdrawn maladjustment	0	0	0		. .
Aggressive maladjustment	1	1	0	0	. .
Talented in drawing	3	1	2	0	1

Perhaps the most interesting fact about the selected children is that there is so little overlapping. If there had been no overlapping membership, there would have been 120 children in the six groups; actually there are 109 children, with five children appearing in two groups, and three children in three groups.

CHAPTER 7

INITIAL COMPARISON OF EXPERIMENTAL
AND CONTROL GROUPS

In an experimental study such as this one, special
care must be taken to define the experimental and the control groups and to make sure that the two groups are substantially alike in all respects except the differences introduced by the experiment ($\underline{1}$). The problem of defining
the two groups is complicated by the fact that some children are continually leaving the community while others
are coming in, so that, to a limited extent, the experimental and the control groups may have shifting populations.

This chapter will define the two groups and describe
the procedures used initially to compare them. Furthermore,
a method of dealing with problems of "contamination" will
be described.

Two groups of children are being studied, one for experimental purposes and the other for purposes of control.
A strict definition of these two groups is given below.

The Experimental Group

Basically the experimental group is composed of children who were in the fourth grade in the public schools in
1951-52. Thus, most of this group were born in 1942.

Not all the children included in the experimental
group were in the regular fourth-grade classroom of the
public schools. Of the children in the educable mentally
handicapped room (EMH Room) in 1951-52, the project included in the experimental group only those born in 1941. This
exception was made on the assumption that all these children would be retarded at least one year if kept in their
regular grade. Pupils in crippled children's classes (CC
Room) in 1951-52 were included if they were born in 1942
or if they were born in 1941 and had an intelligence quotient below 90, on the assumption that the latter are retarded one year. Children in sight-saving classes (SS Room)
who were born in 1942 were included in the experimental
group.

Children from the fourth grade of a local private boys' school and the Lutheran parochial school were included as part of the experimental group.

Out-migrants.--The records of children in the experimental group who move out of the city are put in a special file. Some will return to this city and re-enter the study. In any case, we shall know what portion of children leave the community during the study and what portion of these had been screened out as potentially maladjusted or potentially talented.

In-migrants.--In general, we will add to the experimental group all children who were in the fourth grade in 1951-52 and who enter school here from out of the city in future years. We will add in-migrants to the experimental group and note the year they arrive until the group reaches the age of sixteen, the school-leaving age. After that, we cannot hope to get all names of in-migrants. In-migrants aged 14-16 will probably not be helped much by our study, but we should keep an eye on them, especially as they contribute to delinquency figures.

In-migrants will be screened during their year of arrival and added to the special group if they belong there, at least until the children in the experimental group reach the age of fourteen. We may not want to try treatment of children who enter the community after this age.

The Control Group

The same criteria of inclusion and exclusion are applied to the control group made up of children in the sixth grade in 1951-52. This group consists mainly of children who were born in 1940.

Social Background of the Groups

The two groups of children were compared to find out whether they were equivalent in terms of family socioeconomic status. If they are not of very similar social backgrounds, they cannot be considered comparable groups for the purposes of the study. If they are fairly similar in socioeconomic status, we have some grounds for believing, not only that they can usefully be compared in this study, but also that they are representative of children in this particular community and in other American midwestern com-

munities. If, in addition, they prove to be similar in social background to children of other communities, we have
even better grounds for believing that findings in this
study can be generalized and applied in other cities.

Socioeconomic status was determined by methods developed by Warner (2). Briefly, this method consists of obtaining for the family of each child a numerical score or
index which expressed its socioeconomic position in the
community. This score, called the Index of Status Characteristics (ISC), is determined by the scores on four sub-
indices. These sub-indices, which indicate the social position of the child's family, are (1) type of house in
which the child lives, (2) area of the city in which he
lives, (3) occupation of the father, and (4) source of income of the father.

A seven-point scale was set up for each of the sub-
indices, and a given child was rated on each. The scores
on the sub-indices were weighted, and the total ISC score
was obtained by adding the weighted scores of the sub-
indices.

House-type.--The size and condition of the house were
the two main criteria used in rating a given house on a
scale from 1 (best) to 7 (worst). The estimated size of
the house was based on the number of rooms it contained.
The number of rooms was estimated by the style of the house
and its outside dimensions. A house of 1-5 rooms was considered small; 6-9 rooms, medium; 10 or more, large.

In judging the condition of a house, four factors were
rated: the structural condition of the house (the condition of foundation, chimneys, roof, pillars, walls); the
repair of the house (the condition of the paint, screens,
railings); the landscaping or setting of the house (the condition of the hedges, lawns, fences); and the general aesthetic appeal of the house. Admittedly, these factors are
often difficult to rate, and therefore an understanding of
the housing standards of the community is important. The
executive secretary of the commission, a long-time resident,
helped establish the criteria of condition and helped interpret the housing in the community. On the basis of these
factors of condition, it was found possible to rate houses
as "good," "medium," "poor," or "very poor."

In order to make the procedure of house typing as objective as possible the grid in Table 12 was developed, based on the size and condition of the houses.

In practice, the size and the condition of the house were first determined. The actual rank of the house was thereby automatically limited to the numbers shown within the cells of the table. Large houses could receive a rating from 1 to 7, but small houses only 3 to 7 unless they were in unusually good condition. Age of the house was not used systematically as a criterion of condition since most of the homes in the community were old and varied widely in size and condition. The final rank was determined by further consideration of the condition of the house.

TABLE 12

House-Typing Chart

Number of Rooms	Condition			
	Good	Medium	Poor	Very Poor
10+	1	2 3	4 5 6	7
6-9	2	3 4	5 6	7
1-5	3 4	4 5	5 6	7

Many of the large homes were subdivided into apartments, but apartment buildings as such were rare. No special rating was set up for apartment buildings. Rather, the number of apartments in the building was determined by the number of mailboxes, doorbells, or electric meters on the building. From this information the size of each apartment was estimated. The size of the apartment, not the size of the total building, was used to determine the rating. This procedure automatically lowered the rating of houses which were subdivided into apartments. This is in line with community estimates of the desirability of living in such dwellings compared with single-family houses.

Area type.--Twenty-six distinguishable dwelling areas were defined within the city. Each was given a rating on a scale from 1 to 7 with the help of the judgment of local real-estate dealers. The frequency distribution of the areas and the per cent of each area in the total city are given in Table 13.

Occupation and source of income.--Information on the father's occupation and the source of income for the family was obtained from the pupil personnel cards of the public schools. Occupation was rated on a scale from 1 to 7 following Warner's classification (2:140-41). Source of income was also rated on a seven-point scale following Warner's classification (2:138-42).

The total score.--Each child was given a rating from 1 to 7 on all four sub-indices. Each rating was weighted according to the following formula: occupation rating, 4; source of income rating, 3; house-type rating, 3; area rating, 2. On this basis, a total Index of Status Characteristics was computed for each child. The ISC scores range from 12 (indicating the highest status) to 84 (the lowest).

TABLE 13

Distribution of Dwelling Areas

Rating	Number of Areas	Per Cent of Total Area in City
1 . . .	3	7
2 . . .	5	9
3 . . .	4	9
4 . . .	4	42
5 . . .	3	8
6 . . .	6	11
7 . . .	1	15

Comparison of Experimental and Control Groups

The experimental group, consisting of 457 children, is slightly larger than the control group, which includes 392 children. The experimental group has sixteen pairs of siblings within it, the control group has twelve pairs. Forty-seven children in the experimental group have siblings in the control group, that is, forty-seven families have a child in each group. These data, plus the data on the number of children in special classes are summarized in Table 14.

TABLE 14

Some Characteristics of Experimental
and Control Groups

Characteristic	Experi-mental Group	Control Group
Number of cases . .	457	392
Pairs of siblings within group . .	16	12
Siblings in opposite group . . .	47	47
Educable mentally handicapped children	12	14
Crippled children .	1	2
Children in sight-saving class . .	2	0

Table 15 gives the distribution of ratings in frequencies and per cent for house type, area, occupation, and source of income for the experimental and the control groups, respectively. The table indicates that the two groups are similar in social backgrounds as measured by the Index of Status Characteristics, since none of the differences between the means of the two groups on the sub-indices is statistically significant. Therefore we have some assurance that they are a good sample of the population of parents with children of school age.

Comparison of Socioeconomic Data with Those in Jonesville Study

In order to throw some light on the question whether this city has a typical distribution according to socioeconomic status, the data of Table 15 may be compared with similar data from Warner's study of socioeconomic status in Jonesville (3: 42-51), a smaller midwestern city of about 7,000 population. Table 16 gives this comparison for house type, occupation, and source of income. (Warner does not give the distribution for area type.)

TABLE 15

Sub-Index Distributions for Experimental
and Control Groups

| Rating | Per Cent of Group Given Rating | | | | | | | |
| | House Type | | Area | | Occupation | | Source of Income | |
	Experi-mental	Control	Experi-mental	Control	Experi-mental	Control	Experi-mental	Control
1	1.1	1.3	3.1	1.5	4.4	3.3	0.0	0.5
2	2.0	2.0	4.8	4.3	7.2	6.1	0.9	0.8
3	4.8	3.1	8.3	7.4	11.4	9.2	10.7	5.6
4	14.7	15.1	41.1	39.5	16.6	10.2	28.2	23.0
5	31.7	27.0	10.1	8.2	29.5	34.7	53.6	60.7
6	32.2	37.0	14.9	16.3	21.2	24.7	1.5	3.1
7	12.0	11.7	16.0	20.2	7.4	8.4	2.2	3.6
Unknown . . .	1.5	2.8	1.8	2.6	2.2	3.3	2.8	2.8
Total number . . .	457	392	457	392	457	392	457	392
Mean rating . . .	5.22	5.28	4.62	4.81	4.59	4.80	4.52	4.75

The mean ratings on occupation and source of income
are very similar for the populations from the two communities, but the mean rating on house type is definitely lower
for Jonesville. Since a lower rating means larger size or
better condition, the Jonesville houses are superior to
those in our sample. But the Jonesville sample includes
practically all the heads of families and the houses in
Jonesville, while our sample includes only the parents of
fourth-and sixth-grade children.

Since the entire population was used as a sample in
Jonesville and a sample of young parents (at least young
enough to have fourth- and sixth-grade children) was used
in the present study, one might conclude that this is the
determining difference. These younger parents are probably
not yet able to afford the size and quality of house in
which they will someday live when their families are larger
and they have reached their maximum financial incomes. This
interpretation is supported by the fact that mean scores of

TABLE 16

Comparison of Socioeconomic Data for
Jonesville and Present Samples

Rating	Per Cent of Group Given Rating					
	House Type		Occupation		Source of Income	
	Jonesville	Present Sample	Jonesville	Present Sample	Jonesville	Present Sample
1	4.1	1.1	5.4	3.9	1.0	0.3
2	21.6	2.0	6.1	7.1	2.5	0.9
3	23.6	4.3	10.3	10.8	18.2	8.9
4	11.5	15.2	22.7	13.3	23.2	26.0
5	12.3	29.8	15.1	31.7	53.6	56.2
6	21.6	33.8	21.8	23.0	0.5	2.4
7	3.2	11.7	15.5	7.5	1.1	2.5
Unknown . . .	2.3	2.0	3.1	2.7	0.0	2.8
Total number . . .	2,095	788	2,095	788	2,095	788
Mean rating . . .	3.86	5.23	4.69	4.65	4.32	4.60

the sub-indices of occupation and source of income for the
two studies are very similar. Occupation and source of income should vary less with age among adults than does house
type.

It may be supposed that the data from the Jonesville
study indicate that our sample is not representative of the
total population, but it must be recalled that we do not
claim to have an adequate sample of the total population
but rather of the population of people who have children of
school age.

The Problem of Contamination of
the Control Group

"Contamination" refers to the changes that take place
in the control group as a result of inadvertent application
of treatment methods or indirect benefits of the treatment

program to the control group. Contamination works in the
direction of decreasing the possibility of obtaining significant differences between the experimental and the control groups.

Sources of contamination are the following: (1) presence of children from the same family in both groups and
(2) improved general environmental conditions attributable
to the project. In both these cases, some benefits of the
experimental treatment method are received by the control
group. The second type of contamination is controlled as
much as possible by having a control group which is two
years older than the experimental group and therefore
"ahead" of improved general environmental conditions.

A method of utilizing the former source of contamination for additional research is described below.

There are forty-seven pairs of siblings included in
the experimental and the control groups. These forty-seven
pairs of siblings represent approximately 11 per cent of
the total group. In other words, approximately 1 out of 9
children in either group has a brother or a sister in the
opposite group.

The probability of contamination here is obvious. Suppose the forty-seven parents of these siblings are helped
by the project to deal more effectively with their children
in the experimental group. Probably they will deal more effectively with their children in the control group also.
Of course, it is useless and inadvisable to try to prevent
this result.

However, it would be desirable, from the research point
of view as well as from the treatment point of view, to encourage these parents to help both children. By doing so,
a study could be made of the effectiveness of the work which
the project did with parents. Differences between the adjustment of the experimental children and the control children in the same family could be attributed to differences
in effectiveness of the full treatment program versus only
helping parents. Differences between these control-group
children and other children in the control group could be
attributed to differences in helping parents versus no help
at all.

At present, we cannot tell much about the possibilities
in this connection. Presumably, only a small fraction of the

forty-seven pairs of children will be selected for special study and treatment. However, whenever one of the forty-seven pairs of parents does receive help from the Commission, the effect of the help on their control-group children can be studied as well as the effect on their experimental-group children.

Bibliography

1. Havighurst, Robert J., and Others. A Community Youth Development Program. Supplementary Educational Monographs, No. 75. Chicago: University of Chicago Press, 1952. (The final chapter gives a description of the design of the experiment.)

2. Warner, W. Lloyd; Meeker, Marchia L., and Eells, Kenneth W. Social Class in America. Chicago: Science Research Associates, 1949.

3. Warner, W. Lloyd, and Others. Democracy in Jonesville. New York: Harper & Bros., 1949.

PART II.--THE COUNSELOR TRAINING
PROGRAM: THE FIRST YEAR

CHAPTER 8

THE TRAINING PROGRAM

An essential part of the Youth Development Program was
the training of residents in the community for the study of
children and work with children. This training was divided
into two phases: (1) the preliminary phase, which lasted
about nine months before the counselors actually started to
study local children, (2) the "on-the-job" training, which
will continue throughout the project in connection with the
teams' study of, and work with, local children. This chapter will report on the preliminary training program which
extended from September, 1951, to June, 1952.

Seventy-six persons were enrolled in the training program, slightly over half of them being teachers and school
principals, while the others were volunteers or professional workers with children in such organizations as Scouts,
churches, County health department, and social-service agencies. The group met for two hours one afternoon each week.
The meeting time was divided into one hour for presentation
of material in the form of lectures, demonstrations, or
films, and one hour for the study of case material. The
lectures were given by members of the consultant staff or,
occasionally, by guest lecturers. During the hour of presentation the group met as a whole. During the second hour
the counselors met in three subgroups in order to study the
case materials. A staff member served as discussion leader
in each subgroup.

To a considerable extent the training program was based
on methods and principles worked out at the University of
Chicago and elsewhere for the in-service training of teachers in the study of children. But there were notable differences between this program and other in-service training
programs. (1) The training group was made up of persons from
a variety of fields, with teachers constituting only about
half of the total group, and (2) the purpose of the training
program was to prepare its participants for action in a specific youth development project. Thus the program was pointed toward action, and the action might take place almost

68

anywhere in the community--in churches, Scout groups, social agencies, and homes, as well as in schools. A calendar of the first year's training program is given in Appendix E.

The training program can be roughly divided into three types of activities: (1) <u>presentation of scientific principles</u> in the area of child growth and development, personality development, and group dynamics; (2) <u>interpretation of the project</u>--its need, purposes, and methods; (3) <u>opportunities for application of the learnings acquired</u>, through action--discussion of lectures and cases, team participation, role playing.

Presentation of scientific principles took place throughout the training program. Early in the program the staff gave a series of overview lectures, to provide common vocabulary, concepts, and a common background of understanding. Later the lectures dealt with the functions of the teams: team operation, diagnosis, concepts of group dynamics, therapy, and use of the community agencies.

Interpretation of the project occurred most intensively early in the training program. Almost the entire first meeting was devoted to an explanation of the project. Even as late as the spring, the staff explained the screening devices and discussed how the teams fitted into the project.

Opportunities for application were the most difficult to provide on a meaningful basis. In general, the staff attempted to provide experiences that would later be encountered on the project by using case studies, subgroup meetings, team meetings, and demonstration of team problems. A book describing the cases of children of various types who had been studied elsewhere was the principal teaching instrument. Late in the training program the counselors worked with cases of local children selected because of their obvious maladjustment by fourth-grade teachers in the training program.

Several schemes were tried out in the subgroup meetings as means of analyzing and diagnosing the cases. The counselors were asked to make a systematic analysis and diagnosis using <u>recurring patterns</u> and <u>developmental tasks</u> as their frame of reference. Some of the first cases in the case book were taken from <u>Helping Teachers Understand Children</u> (<u>2</u>), and methods of training suggested in this book were employed.

A good deal of time was spent on the process of composing balanced teams. The counselors took part in this process.

A professional library was set up in a section of the public library. The project provided the books for the counselors.

As part of the training program, two "extra-curricular" groups were set up for those who were interested. One group studied play therapy more intensively than did the counselors in the regular training program. The other group studied concepts of group dynamics. These two groups met one night a week for about two months in the winter.

University credit was offered for the training program. Those taking credit for the course were asked to take two examinations and to assist in interviewing community-agency staffs in preparing a community directory for the use of the teams.

Evaluation of the Training Program

The training course was evaluated by the staff and by the counselors participating in the course.

Evaluation by the counselors.--After the training program had been completed, the counselors were sent a list of the training activities which had comprised the training program and a list of evaluative statements. They were asked to match the training activities to the evaluative statements. The statements and the list of training activities with the instructions are given in Appendix F.

When the evaluation questionnaire was sent out, many of the teachers had already left town for summer study, and other counselors in the group were away on summer vacation. As a result, only 43 per cent of the group responded to the evaluation instrument. Fifty per cent of the responses were from teachers. Table 17 gives the evaluation of the training program by the counselors.

The evaluation instrument was so devised as to force the respondents to make some relatively unfavorable judgments by asking them to indicate at least two activities for every evaluative statement. This avoided the usual polite clustering of evaluations on the favorable side and gave an indication of which activities were the least liked.

TABLE 17

Evaluation of Training Program by Counselors

Training Activities**	Per Cent of Counselors Making Statements*			
	1, 4, 7 Satisfying Enjoyable, Instructive Should Be Repeated	2, 5, 8 Almost Forgotten, Less Instructive Needs Improvement	3, 6, 9 Frustrating Confusing Needs Extensive Modification	10 Did Not Attend
A. Lectures in general . .	17.4	. .	. .	. .
B. Lectures on growth of children	9.7	3.9	. .	1.8
C. Lectures on therapy . .	6.9	4.3	8.3	1.8
D. Lectures on group dynamics	3.7	7.5	4.5	1.8
E. Lectures on project procedures	3.5	2.5	3.6	. .
F. Subgroup meetings . . .	4.0	8.0	17.6	. .
G. Team meetings	4.2	4.5	9.7	. .
M. "Extra-curricular" groups	.2	7.0	9.3	30.3
H. Therapy cases	7.2	3.0	5.1	. .
I. Cases of types of children to be studied .	9.5	.7	^.6	. .
T. Local cases	7.7	1.8	1.7	. .
J. Demonstrations	3.3	11.8	4.2	3.6
K. Movies	6.4	7.0	2.2	. .
L. General discussions without instructors .	1.5	10.0	10.1	1.8
S. Consultation with instructor	2.9	3.7	1.7	12.5
N. Reading	5.8	4.1	3.0	5.3
P. Examinations	.7	3.4	5.7	23.2
Q. Studying	2.1	5.0	1.1	5.3
O. Making community contacts	2.4	3.5	1.1	12.5
R. Filling in evaluation forms	0.8	8.4	10.1	. .
Total	99.9	100.1	99.6	99.9

*See Evaluative Statements, Appendix F.

**See Training Activities, Appendix F.

The counselors rated most highly the lectures in general, the lectures on child growth and development, and the case studies of the types of children with which the project would be dealing. Demonstrations and cases of children in therapy rated medium. Subgroup meetings, team meetings, extra-curricular groups, and evaluation procedures were rated the lowest.

Evaluation by instructors and the Professional Committee.--The instructors and several members of the Professional Committee who took the training course wrote up their general evaluation of the training program. No quantitative measures were obtained from them.

The instructors tended to be less critical of the lectures than were the members of the Professional Committee. The latter felt that the lectures should have been better co-ordinated among themselves, with the case material, and with the movies and the reading.

The use of case studies was assumed by all to be good. There was evidence that people became personally involved in the cases, especially in the case of Marian West and in the play-therapy case of Ernest. The cases of Jed (aggressive boy) and Roberta (talented girl) were probably too detailed and presented with too little interpretation to be used effectively so early in the training program as they were.

There was a good deal of criticism of the methods used in analyzing the case studies. The use of developmental tasks as a frame of reference for analyzing and diagnosing needs did not "take" well. Neither did other systematic schemes, such as recurring patterns. The cases may have been rushed too much to permit success of these efforts to establish a conceptual structure. The lack of a conceptual structure for analyzing a case undoubtedly contributed to the feeling of frustration which some of the counselors showed.

There was a difference among the instructors in their evaluation of the subgroup meetings, ranging from feelings that they were successful to feelings that they were primarily frustrating to the counselors. Rotation of instructors among the subgroups was seen as a good procedure, since it gave them a chance to get acquainted with all the counselors and for the counselors to get acquainted with them. Members of the Professional Committee felt that the subgroup meetings were frustrating and confusing to many counselors.

Using cases of local children in the spring was considered a good idea but poorly organized. At that time each of the subgroups was divided into three teams for the study of local children. All the teams met at the same time. Thus, a group of seven or eight counselors was thrown together in a team and told to commence studying a local child after about eight months of a training program. Since the staff had deliberately refrained from organizing the teams with chairmen, secretaries, or other officers, and since no formal procedure had been set up for analyzing a case, this procedure invited some confusion. Nevertheless, the team was given ample opportunity to work out the procedure most satisfactory to its members.

Since each instructor found himself with three teams under his supervision, all meeting at the same time, he split his time among them. Consequently, some teams waited for him to tell them how to proceed while others went ahead and organized their own procedures.

It became clear to all, however, that most of the teams needed more direction than they were getting. Without it, they would not do an adequate job of analyzing the case, recording the data and their discussions, and coming to clear-cut conclusions on what to do in helping the child. This conclusion was not unexpected, since the training period had been relatively short and the staff had deliberately left as much as possible of the responsibility and initiative to the counselors. Such a procedure as this must be expected to result in some milling-around and lack of efficiency at intermediate points in the training program, but it was expected that this disadvantage would be offset by greater personal involvement in the project by the counselors, which would pay returns later on.

Changes in the Counselors

Two instruments were used to obtain data on attitude changes in the counselors which would be attributable to the training program (1). One was a Wickman scale of attitudes toward behavior in children modified into a Q-sort

test. The second was a diagnostic paragraph test. Both instruments were administered to the counselors at the beginning and the end of the first year's training program. At
the time of this writing, these data remain to be analyzed.

Conclusion

Two things are apparent from the experience of the
training program. First, it is very difficult to attempt
to train as large a group as this. One of the persistent
difficulties for the instructors was trying to become acquainted with, and relate personally to, so many individuals in such a short time. Second, it would be wise to
include some sort of practicum or laboratory experience in
which the counselors could deal directly with children, ap-
plying the concepts and techniques they were learning and
reorganizing their attitudes as the experience demanded.
Such a practicum is being included in the second year of
the project through the training program in play therapy.

Although the effect of the training program is difficult to assess--and the difficulties are obvious--still some
of the positive functions that it performed should not be
overlooked. First of all, it brought together a group of
youth workers to be trained to work with children in a different way from that to which most were accustomed. Second,
it provided a symbol for the project and licensed the counselors, so to speak, to do their work. Third, it provided
a basis upon which to organize a number of teams fairly
quickly and to get started on the project.

The best methods of training and of carrying out the
training in a program such as this remain to be determined.
Perhaps from experiences such as those provided in this
project, a general method will evolve whereby communities
and universities can collaborate more closely in meeting
the training needs of communities in the field of youth
development.

Bibliography

1. DeHaan, Robert F. "The Training Program for Community
   Counselors," A Community Youth Development Program, pp.
   43-44. Youth Development Series, No. 1. Supplementary
   Educational Monographs, No. 75. Chicago: University
   of Chicago Press, 1952.

2. Division on Child Development and Teacher Personnel,
   Commission on Teacher Education. Helping Teachers Understand Children. Washington: American Council on Education, 1945. (Supplies a good overview of purposes
   and methods for giving teachers in-service training in
   child study.)

CHAPTER 9

THE FORMATION AND COMPOSITION OF TEAMS

The team of volunteer counselors which sets up an ongoing relationship with the children is the primary social
invention of this project. There was nothing like it in
the experience of the staff, and no descriptions of anything like it were found in the literature of child development and child hygiene. Consequently, the experience of
the project in this area is reported somewhat fully, with
its false starts as well as its successes.

After the first few months of training, a large part
of the training program was devoted to the process of forming teams. From the outset of the project, the goal was to
form balanced teams, that is, teams having represented on
them all the skills, professions, and interests necessary
to do the task of studying and helping the children assigned
to them.

Method of Composing Groups

The most direct method of composing teams would have
been for the consultant staff simply to assign the counselors to teams. This method was rejected because it was felt
that the counselors should have a part in the process in
order to find teams that enjoy working together.

The staff thought that the counselors would gain a better understanding of the operation of their teams if they
had a part in composing them. The part that the counselors
played was to decide which persons they wished to work with
and what "roles" they could most effectively take on a team.
Each counselor was asked to make a first and second choice
among five roles: analyzer, planner, executor, recorder, and
team facilitator. These roles were defined in an illustrated lecture in a seminar meeting in February, 1952. One of
the counselors, a commercial artist, illustrated the lecture
with large cartoons depicting each role in humorous fashion.

The analyzer was described as the person who fits together the pieces of information about a child to make an
understandable picture. He forms a theory about a child.

76

The planner was described as a person who thinks about what can be done for a child and about the order in which the various steps shall be taken. He visualizes the work of the analyzer in terms of action. He can point out the people who can help children.

The executor function was described as a function to be carried out by persons who have had actual experiences working with and for children in the community. From such persons come those who can establish a therapeutic relationship with the child.

The team recorder was described as the person who keeps written accounts of the team's action. He records data systematically, looks up information, and handles the administrative details between the team and the consultant staff and among the team members.

The team facilitator was described as the person who is sensitive to the problems that the team is having. He helps members clarify their position and tries to maintain a climate in which every person can feel free to participate.

The staff also asked each counselor to name two other counselors with whom he would work well on a team. For his second choice at least, he was asked to name a person from outside his own profession. The counselors were also given a chance to name any persons with whom they did not wish to work.

Balanced Subgroups

With the information on the choice of roles, choice of teammates, and the profession of each counselor, the staff set about to form three subgroups from which nine balanced teams could later be drawn. The formation of balanced subgroups was an intermediate step between the subgroups which had been set up at the beginning of the training program, by dividing the counselors alphabetically by name, and the formation of the final balanced teams.

Table 18 shows the composition of the three balanced subgroups by sex, profession, and first choice of roles. This table indicates a low ratio of men to women. The least popular choices of roles were team facilitator and recorder.

TABLE 18

Composition of Balanced Subgroups by
Profession, Team Role, and Sex

	Subgroup A	Subgroup B	Subgroup C
Profession:			
High-school teachers	5	5	6
Elementary-school teachers	9	8	8
Educators*	1	1	1
Nurses	3	3	3
Board and staff members of social agencies . . .	4	4	5
Scout Leaders and religious educators	3	4	3
Team role choice:			
Analyzer	5	5	6
Planner	5	5	4
Executor	7	6	7
Facilitator	. .	1	1
Recorder	2	2	3
Undecided	6	6	5
Sex:			
Women	20	19	20
Men	5	6	6
Number in group .	25	25	26

*Includes a professor from the local college
and two administrators from the public schools.

In forming balanced subgroups, the staff was able to
put together all the counselors who made mutual choices
and to satisfy about half of the nonreciprocated choices.
Those who said they would work with anyone were placed in
the subgroup where they seemed to fit best from the point
of view of professions or roles.

The balanced subgroups worked together for a period of
about one month in the early spring of 1952. Each subgroup
began the study of a child who was referred to it by one of
the fourth-grade teachers in the training program. This
period of work provided an opportunity for the counselors
to think about their participation in terms of the five
roles and to become better acquainted with one another.

Balanced Teams

In determining the final composition of the teams, it was decided that the counselors' sociometric choices should be considered first, equal distribution of professions next, and equal distribution of choice of roles last.

The staff set up nine teams composed of seven to nine persons each. The composition of the teams by profession, role, and sex is given in Table 19.

TABLE 19

Composition of Balanced Teams by Profession,
Team Role, Sociometric Choice, and Sex

	Number on Team								
	A-1	A-2	A-3	B-1	B-2	B-3	C-1	C-2	C-3
Profession:									
High-school teachers	2	2	..	1	2	1	2	2	1
Elementary-school teachers	2	4	5	3	2	2	2	2	3
Educators	..	..	1	..	..	1	..	..	1
Nurses	1	1	1	1	1	1	1	1	1
Board and staff members of social agencies	2	1	1	1	1	..	1	2	1
Scout Leaders and religious educators	1	..	1	1	1	2	1	1	1
Team role:									
Analyzer	1	2	2	1	2	2	2	3	2
Planner	..	3	2	2	..	3	..	2	1
Executor	3	2	2	3	2	1	2	2	2
Facilitator	..	..	..	..	..	1	..	..	1
Recorder	1	1	1	1	..	..	1	1	1
Undecided	3	..	2	..	3	..	2	..	1
Sociometric choice:									
Number of mutual choices	..	4	1	4	..	1	2	2	1
Sex:									
Women	7	7	6	5	5	6	5	7	7
Men	1	1	3	2	2	1	2	1	1
Number on team	8	8	9	7	7	7	7	8	8

During the course of the summer and autumn of 1952 it became evident that obtaining balance on a team, in the way that has been described here, is not the most important factor in developing successful teams. Other factors in team operation appear to be equally important, if not more so. One such factor is inclusion on the team of a person or persons who are in direct personal contact with the child. Another is having easy and familiar relations with the school and neighborhood where the child lives. A third is relating to schools in such a way that the work of the team and that of the school is mutually helpful. These and other factors in team operation are discussed at length in later chapters.

CHAPTER 10

COUNSELOR TEAMS AND THEIR FUNCTIONING

The whole Community Youth Development Program is centered on the teams of volunteer counselors and their capacity to serve the youth of the community effectively. The first year of the project was mainly concerned with the selection of the counselors and the beginning of their training. The second year was to see the beginning of work with actual children through the teams, as well as the continuing of the training of the counselors themselves.

Team Membership

None of the teams attempted to hold meetings during the summer months, but at the beginning (October) of the second year, eight of the nine teams were actively at work. After a change in its organization, the ninth team became active two months later. Five team members dropped out of teams between the first and the second year. Of these, one moved out of the city, two felt that they were too busy with other duties and activities, and two dropped without communicating to us the reasons. One person who had moved into the community after the beginning of the project and who had had former professional training in social work was added. This provided a total of sixty counselors, two teams of five, one of six, four of seven, and two of eight members.

The dropping-out of approximately 8 per cent of the counselors during the first year calls for analysis to discover the reasons for the drop-outs and to determine whether such drop-outs are to be expected in succeeding years. No systematic study has as yet been made of those individuals who have dropped from the teams, but several probable reasons for their loss of interest can be cited. First of all, the course of training given in the first year was taken for academic credit by 50 per cent of the course members, credit being given by two universities. A course taught by university staff and giving credit would appeal to many varieties of interests and motivations, and it would be of special interest to teachers who need academic credit to maintain

81

their professional status and to obtain increases in salary.
It seems likely that some persons took the course merely for
the credit or for the information which it supplied and that
they did not have sufficient interest in the work of the
project to continue giving time and effort to it. No hard
and fast commitments were asked of people before they took
the course, because it was thought to be preferable that
those not interested should drop out.

On the other hand, it is likely that the course itself
was at fault in not reaching all the students in a more effective way. Comments that "we aren't getting anywhere" or
that "I can't see what good this is doing" were heard both
from those dropping out as well as from those still on teams.
The staff itself felt that the course needed much improvement, especially in the direction of dealing more with problems of working together as a diagnostic team and with techniques of helping children (see chapter 8).

It is expected that some of these persons may return to
the teams with changes in the program or changes in their individual situations and also that there will be less dropping
out in the future since university credit can no longer be a
motivation. At the same time, a certain amount of dropping
out will continue for many reasons, and there must be additional recruitment and training to replenish the teams. The
optimum size of teams remains an open question at this time.

Team Meetings

While the dates of team meetings turned out to be fairly irregular during the autumn months, this situation was
due more to the unsettled state of the project (i.e., training counselors for reporting to parents, beginning play therapy, shifting to area teams) than to irregularities of team
members. Usually, however, teams met twice a month at four
o'clock for an hour to an hour and a half. The preferred
place of meeting was in a classroom at the high school because of its central location and available parking space.
Some meetings were held at the Commission office in order
to have access to files or to the play-therapy room. Teams
experienced considerable difficulty in finding meeting times
suitable to all, because of the wide range of occupations
and working hours of members. Since there were so many
teachers in the group, the after-school hours were chosen.

One or more of the consultant staff attempted to be present at each team meeting, and each consultant met with three teams regularly. There was no formal organization within the team, such as the use of a chairman or secretary. Meetings were always open discussions with voluntary participation. Meeting dates were usually set by the team at the previous meeting, and members were reminded by the Commission office a few days before the set date. Occasionally meetings were called at the initiative of the consultant or one or two members.

A review of the record of these meetings shows three major topics of discussion, in addition to the irrelevant but pleasant social conversation that takes place between people who like to be together. Most of the time was spent in discussion of cases that had been assigned to the team, the topics of discussion being the processes of obtaining and evaluating information, planning action, referring the case to other agencies, and the like. A second major topic concerned the frustrations and difficulties that teams were having in their work. (These eventually proved to be serious enough to warrant changing the basis of the assignment of case loads to teams [see chapter 11].) The third area of discussion was centered on the advisability of changing the team structure and the details of accomplishing the change. All teams were asked to discuss this question at their December meeting.

The role of the consultants relative to the teams has been quite varied. There have been differences in personality of the consultants and their approach to groups, but also the needs of the group have shifted so rapidly as to require shifts in the consultant's role. At times there is need for information that the consultant must provide; mounting frustrations within the group call for initiative from the consultant as a group "therapist." At times he can be truly a consultant on child development.

Seminar Meetings

In addition to the meetings of the individual teams, all the teams met together in a general session once a month. These meetings were the natural carry-over of the weekly class meetings of the first year in their meeting time and meeting place, but their content was of a differ-

ent nature. Five of these meetings were held during the
first five months of the second year. Then they were discontinued as a regular activity in favor of more frequent
meetings of the individual teams.

The general meetings served several purposes. First
of all, they provided a means of regular communication between teams and between the staff and team members. Second,
they provided an opportunity for discussion of problems common to all the teams, and for some group action on them.
The topics that were discussed and acted upon involved a
number of issues.

The first problem discussed was the method of assigning the ninety selected children to the nine teams. Several proposals were made: (1) that a team representative
should go over the list and select its own cases, (2) that
children from one school should be assigned to one team,
(3) that children should be assigned arbitrarily from an
alphabetical list, (4) that they should be assigned by
types of problems presented, and (5) that they should be
discussed by the whole team and assigned. The decision was
to assign them arbitrarily, but this decision was later revised.

A second general discussion concerned the relation of
the teams to parents (see chapter 13). Finally, several decisions were made: (1) parents should be brought into part-
nership with the project as much as possible, (2) the results of the testing program should be reported to the parents of all the children, (3) members of the teams and
staff should prepare themselves to do an adequate job of reporting to the parents. One entire meeting of the seminar
was given over to the role playing of interviews with parents, and at another meeting the tests and test profiles
were studied in preparation for interviewing the parents.

A third major issue was the reorganization of teams
on an "area" basis rather than the original arbitrary basis.
The discussion of possible methods of reorganization occupied half of one meeting, and the mechanics of the reorganization occupied another full meeting.

Difficulties in Team Functioning

In September a list of ninety children from the experimental group was divided up more or less arbitrarily into

nine groups of ten children each. Half of these children had
shown high intellectual ability on the screening tests of
the previous year, and half had shown signs of maladjustment.
To each team was given as great a variety as possible, that
is, a mixture of talented and maladjusted children, children
from a number of different schools and areas of the city, and
a balance of boys and girls. This method of assigning cases
was preferred at the outset by the majority of the counselors, but it led to difficulties that soon required a change.

This system meant that, in the course of its work, each
team would be visiting six to eight different schools and
classrooms and teachers. Conversely, it meant that each
teacher might be visited by seven to nine different persons
from different teams. In practice it also meant that the
team members in visiting a teacher were mainly interested
in a particular child and usually did not think to take
time to interpret to the teacher what the study was all
about. As a result, several teachers became dissatisfied
and irritated at "being bothered." One teacher commented,
"I don't understand why you want to study him. I have a
dozen worse than he is." Above all, it was obvious that
the project did not seem to be of help to teachers and principals, and in some cases was almost a burden.

In addition, there was some suspicion of the teams and
what they were trying to do. Such remarks as the following
were made: "I don't see what they can do. They aren't any
more expert in work with children than we are; why should
we expose the children to them?" Or, "We can certainly
handle any problems we have in this school; we have many
qualified teachers here." Or, "If we need any help, we will
call on the Institute for Juvenile Research (which holds a
clinic in the city every three months) and get expert help."

Most of the teams found also that they would have some
children with whom they had no means of natural contact; they
knew nothing of the school or neighborhood the children came
from, they did not know the teachers or principals or scout
leaders or Sunday-school teachers or nurses. This made it
difficult to get contact with such a child, especially in
any natural way, and it was difficult for a team to maintain
interest in someone whom they knew so indirectly. To attempt
to develop such contacts in a neighborhood meant that each
team would have to do so in from three to five different areas.

Other difficulties arose from a concept established early in the project: that it would be best if the child and his parents did not know that a team was interested in, and working for, a particular child. At the beginning of the year the teams were quite tense about their relationship to parents of the experimental group. How were they to keep their interest in a child from the child and from his family and yet do an effective job of giving him additional help? How would the parents feel when and if they did find out? How could you help children without helping parents? Was all this apparent secrecy necessary? If a family did not want anybody to talk with the child, what could a team do then? On the other hand, if parents were advised of the team's interest, would not this be misinterpreted by many parents and cause fear in some and boasting in others? What would other parents think whose children were not selected for study?

Another serious difficulty to many counselors was their lack of confidence in their own skills to be able to help a child, and their corresponding strong desire for further training before they dealt with an actual "problem child" or "talented" one.

In attempting to alleviate some of these difficulties, three specific actions were undertaken which will be described in more detail in a later chapter: (1) teams were realigned to take their cases from one geographical area of the city centering around a school district, (2) a program was developed of conferring with the parents of every child in the experimental group to report on test findings and ask if they wanted us to help their child in any way, and (3) a training program in play therapy and counseling was begun for a small group of interested persons.

CHAPTER 11

THE FORMATION OF AREA TEAMS

In response to the difficulties that teams were experiencing, the staff began to consider other possible ways of organizing the counseling teams that might have fewer inherent difficulties and frustrations for the team members. Several different proposals were made, each with advantages and disadvantages.

The existing "all-city" team organization had the advantage of giving all teams an opportunity to know the city community as a whole and to work in all the school areas. It had the further advantage that one team was able to follow each of its cases anywhere they might move, as long as they stayed in the city and in the study. It allowed for some flexibility and choice in the team's case load. On the other hand, it led to considerable overlapping between teams; it tended to overlook children who needed aid but who were not shown up by the instruments used; it spread teams so thin that they had no natural ties to schools and neighborhoods; it increased the work of the teams because of the necessity of traveling to many different areas of the city; and it proved to be somewhat of a burden to teachers.

Possible Realignments

It would be possible to assign one team to a specific geographical area of the city and give the team responsibility for all the cases in that area. There were a number of considerations to recommend this procedure: a team would have a continuing relationship to the schools, the teachers, and the community leaders of that area; as each area would have different types of problems, the teams would come to know and understand these differences; the team could get better acquainted with parents and could observe all the children of the experimental grade; the team could concentrate its interest and responsibility so that the members would be freer to exercise their own initiative; perhaps the teams, in addition to studying individuals, could study and take action on problems in the environment of the children.   But assigning the teams on a geographical basis also could mean unequal case loads for teams, too close identification of a team with a city district or with the school where they were located, and difficulty in transferring cases from one team to another as families changed their residence or as children moved from elementary to high school.

We considered the possibility of forming ad hoc teams for each child to be worked with. This arrangement would bring together persons who knew the child and would be likely to have high interest in him, but it would not give a continuing responsibility, would require considerable recruitment and training of personnel, and would undoubtedly be unwieldy to administer.

Some favored the idea of "specialty" teams; that is, one team might specialize in working with withdrawn children, another with gifted children, another in play therapy, another in working with teachers. The team members would thus become more expert in some of their techniques and understanding, and we might be able to make better use of the personnel we had. But, again, this arrangement would mean that teams would have to be reorganized to bring together people of like rather than diversified interests. It would probably mean overlapping or neglect in following through on individual children or the organizing of special teams to take on the follow-up responsibility. The arrangement apparently would work against our basic aim of working with a child as a unified being.

These various possibilities were discussed with a number of individuals, and with the Professional Committee at a special meeting called for this purpose. The consensus was that area teams offered more advantages and that it would be wise to organize one team on an area basis experimentally and to compare its operation with that of existing teams. The idea was later presented to the seminar meeting of all the teams, and there was a strong response in favor of the idea and in favor of immediately adopting this organization for all teams.

Survey of Teams and Individuals

However, action was postponed for one month, until the December training seminar meeting. In the meantime, teams

and staff were to study the matter more carefully. The team
members at their next meeting discussed the question whether
they as a team would prefer to work in a particular area of
the city instead of spreading over the entire city and, if
so, what area they would prefer as their working district.
Seven of the nine teams decided definitely that they preferred the area basis, one was not ready to decide, and one
preferred the existing arrangement.

In addition, the staff undertook to survey by telephone
the individual members of teams to determine any peculiar
individual interests or preferences. Approximately three-
fourths of the counselors were reached and were asked eight
questions. No one answered all the questions, but the data
in Table 20 are at least suggestive of the opinions of teams
about several important team issues. In Questions 1 and 3
it will be noted that no one opposed the area-team idea and
no one saw disadvantages for himself in working in the chosen area. However, 40 per cent of the respondents mentioned
that a major danger to be avoided was too close identification of a team with a school or the school system. Apparently, they felt that part of the genius of the project was
its community nature and that it should remain independent
of the school in order to serve better both the school and
the home. Most outstanding was the fact that every team
member wanted to stay on the team with which he was already
working, although many mentioned that they would be glad to
change if it would be better for the project. There was
very little reluctance to give up cases already assigned,
undoubtedly because so little had been accomplished during
the two or three months since the cases had been assigned.
Two persons preferred to work with withdrawn children, and
two with talented children, but most wanted to work with a
variety of childhood problems. Most were too busy to take
on other activities, but five were interested in play therapy.

The results indicated that the team members were
strongly in favor of shifting to an area case load immediately and that they saw few serious dangers in doing so.
For many of the counselors and staff, this seemed to be
the only step that offered some hope of making it possible
for teams to work in more satisfying ways. In theory, it
seemed clear that a team working in one geographical area

and with one school could do a far better job of working co-
operatively with school personnel and of helping local people to be sensitive to problems and encouraging them to action than could a team working in several areas and with sev
eral schools.

TABLE 20

Opinions of Team Members concerning
Team Reorganization

Question	Frequency of Answer			
	Yes	No	Don't Know	Don't Care
1. Do you approve of the idea of your team working in one city area?	13	..	3	3
2. Do you see advantages for yourself in working in the district your team has chosen?	8	8	..	..
3. Do you see disadvantages for yourself in working in the area your team has chosen?	..	10	2	..
4. Do you prefer to work in the area that your present team has chosen?	10	1	5	1
5. Do you prefer to stay with the team you are on rather than move to another?	13	..	..	4
6. Are there any cases you would be reluctant for your team to give up to another team? . . .	2	14	..	..
7. Is there any type of case you would prefer to work with? . .	4	14	..	..
8. Would you like to take part in any other activities of the project (play therapy, etc.)? .	5	6	1	..

On the other hand, the procedure was untried, and some
felt that the existing arrangement should be given a longer
trial. Certainly, if a change was to be made, it should be
carefully done so as to maintain team morale. The sensible
course of action seemed to be to try it out experimentally
before shifting all teams. We knew that, whatever the decision, we would have to live with it for some time to come;
but the mounting difficulties were calling for action.

The Mechanics of Realignment

The results of the survey and the team decisions were
presented to the December seminar meeting for action. Teams
sat as teams during the meeting and made their final decision. It was unanimous in favor of proceeding on an area
basis. Teams then finally settled on their preference of
area and on their regular time and place of meeting. The
first bit of team organization occurred when each team selected one member to be the liaison person; this person
would be the means of communication between the office and
the team, between the school and the team, and among various
team members. After the realignment was complete, time was
given for individuals to shift teams, and two shifts were
made. At the end of the seminar meeting the reorganization
had been completed, and teams were ready to operate on the
new basis at their next meeting in January.

New Role of Teams

How this shift in organization of teams will affect
their functioning in the community is difficult to foresee.
Their main purpose remains the same: to help the selected
children, teachers, and parents to better development of
youth. However, the area organization gives them a more direct contact with the environment, and it brings them into
direct contact with the children and adults. It makes it
more possible for teams to take action aimed at changing the
neighborhood environment, if they discover situations that
are making it difficult for youth in that area. It gives
them an opportunity to establish long-term contacts with
persons in the area, and this can make possible gains for
others than the experimental group. All this does not de-
tract from the job of studying individual children but rather enriches its possibilities.

CHAPTER 12

THE PLAY-THERAPY PROGRAM: TRAINING
AND TREATMENT

The counseling teams were originally set up with the idea that they would rely on existing agencies in the community for the resources needed in helping children. It soon became apparent, however, that the community resources in the area of psychotherapy were insufficient to meet the needs uncovered by the teams. The only agency in the city offering this kind of service was the Family Service Agency. This agency was doing a creditable job, but its case load was well filled and its budget under the Community Chest was too limited to allow much expansion. The problem of the Commission was how to provide the needed therapeutic services without duplicating the work of other agencies in the community and, at the same time, develop interest and support for enlarging the services of the existing agencies.

There were also requests from several individuals and agencies for training in the field of therapy for various professional people working with children, such as school counselors, nursery-school teachers, and others. Requests from several team members for training in therapy have been previously mentioned.

In addition, there was a feeling among many team members that not much can be done to change children, a "you-have-to-show-me" attitude about such things as therapy. Some first-hand experiences in personality change seemed to be needed to give the teams confidence that the job which they had taken on could be accomplished.

Why A Play-Therapy Program?

These needs, in the minds of the staff, added up to the advisability of undertaking a training program in play therapy. A number of considerations were involved in the choice of play therapy as a Commission activity.

Play therapy is one of the most important methods of helping emotionally disturbed children reorganize their personality and function on a more adequate level. Play is the

natural expression of the child's emotional life, and it is
adaptable to use by various theoretical approaches to psychotherapy. Unstructured play in the presence of a sensitive and understanding adult has been proved by many clin-
ical investigators to be effective therapy for children
(see references at end of chapter).

Most effective play therapy seems to have been done
with children below the ages of twelve or thirteen. Since
most of the children we are working with are now ten and
eleven, play therapy might seem to be of limited value to
our program. However, it could undoubtedly be of help to
many of our children, and the earlier it could be put into
operation, the greater would be its effectiveness.

Other advantages of play therapy recommend it for a
training program for teams and agencies. Unlike therapeutic
work with adults, therapy with children can be observed by
conscientious, professional people without violating confi-
dences of the persons involved, since most of the communication is through play rather than spoken, intimate information. It is also fairly simple to make the physical arrangements for observation. A special one-way vision glass is
placed in one wall of the playroom. To the occupants of the
playroom the glass looks like a mirror, but people in the
adjoining room can see through it and observe clearly the
activity in the playroom. With the aid of a microphone, am-
plifier, and loud speaker, they can also hear what is being
said. This arrangement provides a much more dynamic learning situation than do notes or recordings of the interview.

The results of play therapy can usually be seen graphically and often very quickly and thus provide a rather con-
vincing demonstration to observers that children can change
and that the direction of the change can be influenced by
skilful therapists. While, for many persons, work with
children is less threatening than work with adults, it does
force those participating in it to examine their own personality and their approach to other people in a most effective way.

It was finally decided to undertake a play-therapy program, and a playroom and observation room were set up at the
offices of the Commission. It was understood that this was
primarily a training project and that the treatment would be

limited to the experimental group of children. There was
some reluctance on the part of the staff to locate the
room at the Commission offices, since the Commission did not
want to become identified as a service agency, but there
seemed to be no better place. Some felt that locating the
room at the Board of Education might bring confusion with
the special-education rooms there. Space was offered in
elementary schools, but their location away from the center of town and the difficulty of having an observation
room in a school discouraged this type of location. Space
was available at the Commission office; it was convenient
to the participants; and it could better be controlled and
supervised in a training program.

The hope and expectation are that, as the participants
become skilful in the use of play therapy, they will set up
their own facilities at their places of work or adapt what
they learn to various forms of group work and social milieu
therapy.

The Training Groups

A word-of-mouth invitation to teams and to community
agencies brought to the office approximately fifteen persons
who wanted to give several hours a week to training in play
therapy. Seven of these were teachers who could not meet
during the day, and at this writing their group is being organized for an out-of-school hour. Eight persons were from
the staffs of various agencies who could meet during the
daytime hours. This group started work on October 17, 1952,
and has met regularly for two hours or more on Friday afternoons. It is made up of two public health nurses, two school
counselors, a nursery-center teacher, a director of a children's home, a Commission staff member, and two social workers. These people are all engaged in work with children,
and a few have had experience in therapeutic work.

The first two afternoons were spent in general discussion of play therapy and the introduction of a shelf of reading material available in the office. At the third meeting
one of the school counselors brought into the playroom a
child with whom he had been working at school. Since that
time three other children have been referred for therapy,
and members of the training group have worked with them as
counselors. These cases include one child who is a disturb-

ing behavior problem in his schoolroom and is a difficult
problem to his teacher. Another is withdrawn to the point
of engaging in regressive, solitary play and being very shy
in school. Another is a very "good" boy in school but his
mother is concerned about his low grades. Another, referred
by his teacher, had an emotional outbreak in the classroom,
with crying and vomiting. The time is too short to note any
changes except in the first boy, in whose case both the
teacher and the principal have independently reported improvement in school behavior.

During the Friday afternoons, three children are usually seen for thirty minutes each. Another half-hour between
sessions is spent in discussing what has happened. These
discussions take the form of noting various perceptions of
what the child was trying to express, of exchanging observations about the feelings and performance of the therapist
(who is always in the discussion), and of discussion of what
is known of the child from other situations. Five of the
group have indicated that they are ready to try the role of
therapist, two of whom have never had any previous experience in this field. It should be noted that the instructor
has purposely avoided acting as therapist for observation
by the group, believing that this makes it easier for a
learner to take the step of counseling his first case for
observation. All are at approximately the same level of experience. Experience indicates that, after the first step
is taken, learning can proceed in a very active and interested way and that the instructor can then take his turn in
the group without freezing out participation by others.
Three of the group have requested books on therapy, and recently a discussion was requested on what is the goal of
therapy.

Observational Groups

Several other uses of the observation room have developed. Several teams are trying to bring into the playroom
for one session each child that they study. This session
is not considered necessarily a therapy session, but it
gives the team a chance to become acquainted with the object of their study as a person, as well as to observe his
general behavior. Just the experience of seeing the child
has seemed to remove much of their feeling of distance
from the children who are studied.

Several team members have come in to observe therapy sessions with a child to whose care they were assigned, and they have stayed late afterward discussing what they observed. In two cases recently this led to discussion of personal problems. In addition, several persons who have observed only one play session seemed to be stimulated to considerable constructive thinking about personality and behavior. Two of these have been members of the Commission: one a school principal and two visiting scholars on traveling fellowships.

These facilities have also been offered to several local agencies to use as they need them. It is hoped that the value of therapeutic work, and of means of promoting mental health and wholesome human development in general, can be graphically demonstrated to the community in such a way that a demand for such services will be created.

It is much too early to attempt to evaluate this part of the training and treatment program. Two observations can be made. First, a play-therapy program does stimulate interest and brings a number of people into active relationships with the project. Second, it provides a focus for thinking about therapy and personality problems that seems to force the observers to examine their own feelings and concepts rather thoroughly.

Bibliography

1. Allen, F. _Psychotherapy with Children_. New York: W.W. Norton & Co., 1942.

2. Axline, Virginia Mae. _Play Therapy_. Boston: Houghton Mifflin Co., 1947.

3. Jackson, Lydia, and Todd, Kathleen M. _Child Treatment and the Therapy of Play_. New York: Ronald Press, 1950 (second edition).

4. Klein, Melanie. _The Psycho-Analysis of Children_. New York: W. W. Norton & Co., 1932.

5. Lowenfeld, Margaret. _Play in Childhood_. London: Victor Gollancz, Ltd., 1935.

CHAPTER 13

PARENTS AND THE PROJECT

Fundamental to the operation of the teams is the question: How shall the project deal with the parents of the children it is studying? This question touches on one of the most important relationships of the project.

Two alternatives were apparent to those who thought about the question. First, parents could be by-passed or merely informed of what the teams were trying to do for their children when the parents' co-operation became essential. The children would be treated through environmental manipulation and through therapeutic relationships with team members, or both, without necessarily including the parents in any way. This answer pointed up a dilemma of team operation. The teams were set up to take the initiative in helping children; yet they had no socially acceptable or licensed method of taking the initiative or of offering help to parents of these children.

In the early stages, the teams began to work on the basis of ignoring the parents. Team members, usually teachers or public health nurses, visited the parents to get information on home conditions, relationships between parents and children, and other important aspects of the situation. But this was seen to fall short of a major goal of the project, namely, to be of help to parents in their relations with their children. Considerable dissatisfaction was expressed by team members about their relations with the parents. Some parents were guarded and suspicious in their conversations with team members.

An alternative answer was to include the parents in the program of treatment from the beginning and to consider their co-operation essential to the treatment program for their children. This alternative involved working out a method of communicating with parents in such a way that their concerns about their children plus the skills of team members could be brought together to focus on the best possible treatment for the children.

In October of 1952 the staff and the counselors decid-

ed to follow the latter course. When this decision had
been made, a great deal of anxiety on the part of the team
members was relieved. It was evident that they had been
concerned about the prospect of working with children without the consent, or at least the knowledge, of the parents.

The next question followed naturally: What kind of
help can the project offer parents? Since the proffered
help must be socially acceptable to them, it could not ordinarily be help that was based explicitly on the fact of
a child's maladjustment. From the standpoint of the project, however, it had to be the kind of help that could initiate an ongoing relationship with the parents.

Reporting test results to the parents met these criteria. In this way the testing program served more than a
mere screening function, for it also provided a reason for
communicating with parents. Presumably, all the parents
had the opportunity to know about the testing program through
their children's reports from school. The parents were probably curious to know what tests had been given and how well
their children had done on them. It was also assumed that
the parents would have some concern about the development of
their children and that knowledge of the test results might
be of use to them in this respect.

It now became apparent that the project had to deal
with all the parents, not merely with those of the selected
children. Including all parents was desirable for a number
of reasons. There was no way to single out the parents of
the selected children without putting them on the defensive
should they discover that this had been done. Reporting to
all the parents was desirable from the point of building up
the good will of the community toward the project. Finally,
helping some and not others seemed to be unfair if it were
possible to help all.

Since reporting to all the parents had not been done
before and is a time-consuming task, it was decided to experiment in one school and establish a procedure there.

Reporting Test Results

The following procedure was used in reporting to parents
1. The principal of the selected school was asked to
meet with the project staff and the fourth- and fifth-grade
teachers to indicate which parents in the fifth grade (the

experimental group in that school) would be most receptive
to the idea of learning the results of the tests and which
would be the least interested. A half-dozen were named in
each category.

2. Invitations to a planning meeting were sent out by
letter and telephone to the parents whom the teachers considered most receptive. The purpose of the reporting meeting to be held later was explained to them, and various procedures for reporting were discussed. Two dates were set
for reporting meetings so that everybody would be able to
attend. The meetings were to be held in the school in the
evening. The parents decided that principal and teachers
should not be present in case any parent had resistance to
the school. This decision was acceptable to the school personnel.

3. Letters were sent to all the parents via the fifth-
grade children. The letters explained the purpose of the
meeting, gave a choice of dates, and asked the parents to
check the date that would be most suitable for them. There
was also a space to check if they would not be able to attend the meeting but would like somehow to know the results
of the tests. The responses were collected by the teacher.

Table 21 gives the response to this invitation along
with data on the children. There were thirty-one children
in the class. Of these there were two pairs of siblings,

TABLE 21

The First Parent-Report Experiment

Response to Invitation	Total Number of Parents	Number of Parents Responding		
		Withdrawn Children	Aggres- sively Mal- adjusted Children	Intellec- tually Talented Children
1. Will attend first evening meeting . .	6	1	. .	1
2. Will attend second evening meeting . .	8	1	. .	. .
3. Cannot come	13	2	5	. .
4. No response	. .	. .	. .	. .
Total	27	4	5	1

and two new children in the class had not taken the test.
Thus, the total of families to be met was twenty-seven.

The table indicates that a fairly large fraction of
the parents could not come. No attempt was made to find
out why they could not come, and these parents were interviewed later in their homes. All the aggressively maladjusted children and half of the withdrawn children were represented in this group. Seven fathers were present at the
meetings. Seven teams sent one or more counselors to assist with the reporting. Wherever possible, a team member
was assigned to report to the parents of a child with whom
his team was working.

This table represents only the parents of children in
one school. The procedure has not at this writing been
carried out in other schools.

4. A reporting form was prepared which briefly described all the tests and showed with horizontal bars the
child's percentile rank on each test relative to a vertical
line, usually placed near the center of the page, indicating the fiftieth percentile. The profile was so constructed that a line representing the highest score of the child
went all the way to the right-hand margin, even if that
score was no higher than the fiftieth percentile (in which
case the fiftieth percentile was entered vertically near
the right-hand margin). For children with high scores, the
ninety-fifth percentile on any test was indicated by a second vertical line near the right-hand margin. Thus, the
profile for every child indicated his relative strengths
and weaknesses but did not bring out glaringly the position
of the child relative to the total group. Examples of profiles of children with high and low scores are given in
Appendix A.

5. A short training program, of two meetings, was set
up for team members who were to do the reporting. Team
members chose the parents to whom they were to report. The
training program acquainted them with the test materials
and with any background data that they desired on the child
to whose parents they were to report. The team members
role-played the "reporting situation" in order to improve
their skills, not only in conveying the facts of the tests,
but also in understanding the concerns of the parents.

This training emphasized that the project was interested in being of help to parents in planning for their
children, as distinguished from getting information from
the parents or advising them what to do. The training also
emphasized that the parents' perceptions of their children
were as valid as the tests and were needed in order to give
a well-rounded picture of the child.

5. The reporting meetings began with introductions by
everybody, although most of the parents knew one another.
The team members were introduced as counselors. Each parent was given a written list of the tests with an explanation of each (see Appendixes B and C). A staff member reviewed the purposes of the tests, gave a brief statement of
their general nature, and asked for questions. After a
short discussion, each parent or pair of parents went with
a counselor to a room in which the conference was to be
held. The counselor put the reporting form on the table
for the parents to inspect and, from then on, followed their
lead.

7. The parents and counselors gathered again as a group
following the individual conferences. This session provided
the opportunity for parents to bring up any matters which
they thought might be of interest to the whole group.

8. Individual interviews in the homes followed the same
pattern as the conferences described above.

9. Each counselor wrote a report of his conference. The
following reports are typical.

Interview with Mr. and Mrs. E. (in the Home)

Mr. E. answered the door and invited me to come in if
I didn't mind exposing myself to the flu, which he had at
the time. He appeared to be about in his middle fifties.
We sat down in the living-room and waited for Mrs. E. to
finish a telephone conversation. The room was very neat,
and much consideration had apparently been given to its
decoration. One wall was papered differently from the other walls in accord with the present vogue. The windows had
maroon drapes with a floral print. Wallpaper was also maroon. The radio was playing loudly in the dining-room ad-
jacent.

After he had turned off the radio, Mr. E. and I began
to talk. After covering what it was like to have the flu,
I mentioned how convenient their house was to the school
and how nice it must be to have the schoolyard for the kids
to play in. Mr. E. said that they only played over there
when they had organized games, and usually all the children

came to his yard to play in. "We ought to have gravel or macadam instead of grass. You can never keep any grass growing in our yard." When, in the course of the conversation, I asked whether this city had always been his home, he told me how he had lived here since age eight and that his father, grandfather, and great-grandfather had all lived here. He went into quite a bit of detail as to the size, location, etc. of his great-grandfather's farm.

Mrs. E. joined us and sat in a chair beside her husband. I took another chair and moved closer to them. I introduced the profile sheet and held it out to them. Mr.E. took it and looked at it without sharing it with Mrs. E. I asked her if she'd like to move her chair over so that she could see it, but she made no move.

After looking it over briefly, he handed it back to me. I passed it to his wife. Mr. E. said, "How can they test aptitudes in nine-year-olds?" He didn't have much confidence in the tests. "On this social confidence I see Ed did very poorly, but he's the friendliest kid you ever saw. If this were for Ed's younger brother, it would be just right. They are exact opposites." Mrs. E. concurred.

After a pause, I asked, "How is Ed making out in school?" Mr. E. answered, "Well, getting by, I guess you could say. He's smart enough, but he just isn't interested in that sort of thing. I suppose he'll make out all right, though."

At this point Mr. E. wanted to know all about the Youth Development Commission. I satisfied his curiosity as best I could. At one point, while I was talking about the project being of help to families, Mr. E. said, "Well, a family is really a problem, and it'll keep right on being a problem."

"Now this Youth Development is something new in kids that I didn't know about," Mr. E. said.

"When we were kids," said Mrs. E., "we just had to take the bumps by ourselves." I asked if there was any way in which they felt they would like the project to work with them in regard to Ed. Mr. E. answered, "No, I can't think of any way he could use help. He gets along fine with the other kids, seems happy, and so forth. He's not doing too well in school, but I think he'll get past that somehow. We'll keep it in mind though." A little later he added, "Of course, you can never know just what kids are thinking."

As Mr. E. let me out the door, he said that he might come up to the Commission office "to look over the setup."

Interview with Mr. and Mrs. B.
(at the Reporting Meeting)

Mr. and Mrs. B. were not much interested in the profile. They glanced at it and immediately expressed concern over Bill's basic skills, especially arithmetic. Mr. B. said he wants Bill to know everything he needs to know to get a good job when he is finished with school. "I have to use arithmetic all the time on my job [assistant foreman]. Of course,

I learned a lot of mine on the job, but he'll have to know
all these things too if he wants to get a good job."

Mrs. B. wanted to find some way to help Bill with his
school work. "I try to help him, and I can get the right
answer. But he says, 'That's not the way we do it, Mom.'"

Bill is large for his age. His parents sympathize
with him, knowing that people expect more from him than he
is able to deliver sometimes. He is held responsible for
any misdeeds the group does because he is the biggest in the
group.

The parents also were a little troubled because, as
they saw it, the school didn't provide enough supervised
play activity. They want more supervised playground activity for Bill. They hope that the Commission will be able
to be the go-between--for the parents and the school. They
felt the Commission should report its findings to the school
board.

Interview with Mrs. C.
(at the Reporting Meeting)

As Mrs. C. and I walked down the corridor to our conference, she told me about her family. Clare is the oldest
child. Next comes another boy, and then two younger girls.
The youngest is two years old. Then she told me about her
husband and gave me some facts about his family and his
brothers. She was quite talkative.

At the start of the interview I handed the score sheet
to her, and she studied it quietly for a while and then remarked that she was interested and relieved to know that the
test scores were to be given to all the parents. [Profile
shown in Appendix A, No. 2.] She was concerned that perhaps
her child was only one of a few that were selected.

I remarked, "Yes, all the parents are to receive the
results of the test in this same way."

Mrs. C. then began to talk about Clare. Mentioned
that he was a real problem to her. She was concerned because he seemed to resent her and especially his next brother. At first he wanted a sister but, when the brother arrived, he was a very happy little boy. Later he began to
mistreat the brother, and she had to punish him. Now he
openly resents the brother, but he likes his two baby sis-
ters and is good to them.

She says he reminds her of the way she used to feel,
and she is afraid he will have the same feelings as she had.
She was afraid to say what she thought, particularly when
she got to high school. One teacher there made a remark
that she remembers to this day. After that remark she says
she would not volunteer--she knew but just was afraid to
talk.

Then she compared Clare with herself. Told how he liked
to draw and read. She was concerned about his keeping to
himself. She wanted him to have friends but he seemed to be
unable to keep a friend.

Finally, I suggested that she study Clare's aptitude scores. She first remarked about Test 2 [Davis-Eells Games]. She mistook the word "problem," thinking it referred to arithmetic. Then she mentioned the fact that Clare was having trouble with arithmetic and that the principal was giving him special help. Seemed as if he could find the answer but didn't want to bother with learning number facts. She stated that this was the way she used to feel too. I explained that problem-solving did not refer to arithmetic ability but to practical problems and explained what this test meant.

Second, she remarked about the score for Test 6 [Spatial Aptitude]. At first, she interpreted it to mean drawing ability, and I explained it meant other than the ability to draw. She remarked, "Oh yes, the consultant said the drawing scores were not ready." She said she would like to know how Clare rated in drawing because that was one thing he liked to do.

Third, she referred to Tests 13, 10, and 11 [tests of social competence]. Then she told me of several instances which caused her concern.

Then she said, "You know, I'm glad that you were the one to interview me. I like to talk to you and, if one of the others had come with me, I wouldn't have been able to talk to them. You know, I'm timid and I never had any close friends because of that fact." Then she mentioned her concern about Clare and his friends. But she said, "I got along all right finally, and I just know things will eventually work out for Clare, too."

Finally, I suggested that she give the scores a last study and mentioned that she was to feel free to contact the Commission if she felt she needed further explanations. She would like to work with the Commission to help Clare.

I observed that, when she was relating some of the instances of her reactions and Clare's behavior, tears came to her eyes. Then she remarked that Clare was just like her, he cried easily.

On the way back to the conference room she mentioned the fact that her husband had a bad temper at times but that he, too, was concerned about Clare. "Yes," she said, "I have a problem."

Interview with Mrs. J.
(at the Reporting Meeting)

I had met Mrs. J. on a former occasion. She began to talk immediately upon seeing the test scores. [Profile shown in Appendix A, No. 1.]

"Does this mean I.Q.? Looks like she did all right. The verbal is lower than the others. That is the way she is. She is quite different from her sister in many ways. Sister is two years older and takes more after her Dad. Jane takes after me, I guess. She is very quick to get things, and quick to act. Sister takes more time, slower, but she seems to get them, too. Jane is kind of flighty, maybe. She sort of says what she has to say and isn't too

polite sometimes. That's the way I am--say what I have to
say. I'm not proud of it, but that's the way I am. I say
things to the girls that I wish I hadn't, but I always tell
them afterwards I'm sorry for what happened. But it isn't
good for them, and I know it. Wish I didn't do it, but I
don't suppose I could change that much.

"She is pretty high in spatial. What does that mean?
[The team member gave an explanation.] Would that include
such things as designing? She seems to like to do that.
So does her sister. I've tried to give them some advantages along those lines. They both took to music and dancing,
but I couldn't keep them up. My husband was killed in an
accident and I have had to be both mother and father, and
that is pretty hard and I haven't done as well as I should.
But I've tried.

"I'm not worried about either of the girls. Wish I
had more time to be with them, but they seem to get along
pretty well. I may regret some of the things I do later.
These social things seem all right, about average. Pretty
high in leadership--she has ideas all right, usually keeps
me and her sister going."

Interviewer: "Would you be interested in any special
help with Jane in designing or art?"

Mrs. J.: "Well . . . . I might. You see, I want them
to have things, but I can't do too many things on account
of finances.

"How did this commission begin? Dr. Havighurst was
here at the PTA and spoke last year on the gifted child. I
remember one mother asking a question about whether her
child would be taken out of the grade if he was gifted. I
heard the program discussed at two PTA board meetings, but
I really don't understand much about it. But you know this
is a wonderful thing. I've heard some parents talking about
it, just wondering, you know, about the tests and so forth.
Not many of them know anything, but just wondering. It is
good for us to see our child like others see him."

Results of the Reporting Experience

The staff and the team members felt that reporting
test results had bridged the gap between the parents and
project in the school where it was tried. For example,
one of the parents requested further therapeutic help.
Another decided to send her child in for play therapy. In
all cases except one, the counselors felt that they had established a positive relation with the home.

It is interesting to note that none of the parents
gave evidence of being emotionally upset by the test results per se. This may be attributed partly to the fact
that none of the tests were reported as intelligence-test
scores. Rather, the strong points and the weak points were

shown relative to each other, and the emphasis was on the
possible <u>meaning</u> of the profile. Another reason for the
lack of defensiveness or emotionality on the part of the
parents may have been the fact that the profile was used
as a basis for further planning for the child, not as an
end in itself. Also, the information was offered to parents without demanding any action from them. Still another reason may be that in many cases the test results confirmed the parents' observations about their child. In
some cases the parents gave only a cursory glance to the
report form and then began to talk about their own concerns
for their child.

PART IV.--THE COMMUNITY

CHAPTER 14

THE COMMUNITY AND THE PROJECT

The Work of the Community Commission

The second year of the Youth Development Commission continued with the active participation of the Commission as the policy-making group of the project. The Commission met seven times during the year, evening meetings being found more satisfactory than luncheon meetings. The membership remained the same as that in the previous year, with the addition of the state's attorney and a representative from the Negro community. The members were representatives of the following organizations or officials:

    Board of Education
    Boy Scouts of America
    City council of the parent-teachers' association
    The College
    County court judge
    County Health department
    County medical society
    Exchange Club
    Family Service Agency
    Girl Scouts of America
    Kiwanis Club
    Lions Club
    Maternal and Child Health Association
    Negro Community
    Police matron
    Rotary Club
    Service League
    State's attorney
    Welfare Council
    YMCA Board of Directors
    YWCA Board of Directors

Three committees, appointed by the chairman of the Commission, functioned throughout the year. The Budget Committee reviewed and approved for presentation to the Commission the annual budget, as well as items that called for unusual expenditures. The Membership Committee studied the question of additional representation on the Commission and the two new members previously mentioned were appointed. The Publications Committee was appointed to review and approve any articles to be published concerning the progress of the project. The Publications Committee decided that, for the present, the name of the community in which the project is located should not be used in print.

Extension of the Screening Program

Intermittently from the beginning and intensively during the past year, the Commission has felt concern about the extra-experimental implications of the project. The Commission strongly feels that none of its decisions should in any way jeopardize the original project or water down the work being done with the children now within its scope. As yet, the effective counseling load which the presently trained teams can sustain is not known, and the skilled staff provided by the University is still fully preoccupied with the conduct of the project on its original terms. Nevertheless, the Commission is of the opinion that, to be ultimately valid, the experiment must demonstrate that such a project is capable of permanent application in the community

The presence in the community of the pilot project affords a unique opportunity to learn what can be done toward a community-wide application of its assumptions (though these are as yet untested); to wait until verifiable results are obtained will waste much time and deprive many children of assistance which the Commission, by a timely venture of its own, may well be able to provide. This attitude of the Commission is not, in essence, a criticism of the project. Rather, it indicates faith in the ultimate vindication of its assumptions and methods, while also reflecting an opinion that the project as originally devised lacks, perhaps unavoidably, an essential element of final validity: the testing of the possibility of its application on other than a limited and experimental basis.

Assuming, as the Commission does, that the testing methods are significant (either as they are now employed or as they may be modified by experience) and that the counseling program will prove effective, is the whole procedure practicable as a community-wide function on a permanent basis? The Commission strongly feels that, even if the answer to this query should be negative, the project is eminently justified. The Commission believes, however, that this is a highly significant question and that the project is justified in seeking an answer to it if this can be done without danger to the pilot project. Could the Commission sustain the project in the absence of the rather elaborate basis now provided with foundation funds? If foundation funds were not available, to what agencies in the community could we turn for the financing and practical assistance essential to provide skilled direction, train an adequate number of counselors, and operate the project? How could the training program be organized and sustained within the community even if funds were forthcoming? Where would lie responsibility for the testing program--and for co-ordination of all the functions of the project? How many counselors would we have to provide for permanent operation? If the present number is thought necessary to work with one experimental grade, does it follow that an equal number would have to be trained for each grade admitted to the program? What happens to the counseling load of each grade? Does it decrease and, if so, how rapidly? What will be the turnover in counselors? These questions are in addition to the very big question pertaining to general applicability (which we in particular do not have to answer): How would a community initiate the program without a ready-made and providentially supplied pilot project such as we enjoy?

We do not as yet know enough to answer these and many other embarrassingly pertinent questions. But neither do we consider that the answers will arise from speculation. The Commission proposes to find the answers by the application of necessity; for it has decided, after exhaustive discussions at a number of sessions devoted to the problems implicit in its decision, to screen the incoming fourth grade this year, and next year to try to provide the counseling program for this grade as well. It is contemplated, but not yet decided, that the Commission will attempt to extend the screening and counseling program to incoming grades on a permanent basis, the decision each year depending upon the success with which answers to the implied problems are found. Since the funds and machinery now available extend only to the pilot project, it is up to the Commission, not now in possession of financial or technical resources appropriate to the purpose, to execute the expansion of the project without in any way diminishing the original undertaking. It is understood that success or failure in the proposed expansion may go far to provide insight into the missing criterion: community practicability without foundation financing and other outside support.

We do not anticipate that it will be difficult to provide the testing part of the program on a permanent basis. While the present consultant staff has been alert to help, it was early apparent that an increase in the staff must be made, at least for the present. Therefore, upon application of the Commission and with the co-operation of the Board of Education, the foundation extended its assistance to provide an additional staff member for two years. This person was employed in January, 1953, and he will assist the public schools in studying, and in experimenting with the expansion of, their own testing program in the areas covered in the pilot project. The expectation of all concerned is that the testing program now proposed by the Commission will independently justify itself through its value to the school staffs and that, at the end of the two-year period, its proved value will result in its being taken over and effectively administered by the Board of Education.

The extension of the counseling part of the program is patently the more difficult problem. Again, the presence of the existing consultant staff and teams should prove of signal benefit. But the details of providing counseling merely for the new fourth grade now being screened are still under discussion. It may prove possible for the existing teams to carry a major part of the load of this immediate expansion, although this will not be attempted unless it is clearly feasible. But ultimately, despite an anticipated decrease in the case load of each grade, means will have to be found to provide the training program requisite for increasing and maintaining the counseling personnel.

Much interest has been shown in the project by persons outside the community. As a result, a number of visitors have spent from one to several days in the office, attending committee meetings and team meetings and conferring with the staff and the people in the community.

In the summer of 1952 Robert J. Havighurst returned to Chicago, and Paul H. Bowman was appointed chief consultant. Dr. Bowman came from the University of Louisville, Kentucky, and moved with his wife and children to the community in July, 1952. The present staff includes:

> Paul H. Bowman, assistant professor of human development, University of Chicago
>
> Robert F. DeHaan, instructor in human development, University of Chicago

Robert D. King, research associate in human development, University of Chicago

James V. Mitchell, Jr., research associate in human
development, University of Chicago, and specialist
in research in testing in the public schools of the
community

LaVona A. Johnson, executive secretary

The Professional Committee

The Professional Committee has continued in its advisory capacity to the Commission and to the staff on technical
questions which arise in the course of the project. They
have held monthly luncheon meetings, except for the summer
months, with several additional meetings in the fall to discuss the problems of team reorganization. By approval of
the Commission, three names were added to the membership of
the Professional Committee, which now consists of the following:

Executive director, Family Service Agency
Director, Catholic Youth Organization
Director of special services in the public schools
Educational director of the county health department
Teacher of educable mentally handicapped in the
public schools
General secretary, YMCA
General secretary, YWCA
Chairman of the department of education at the
college
Executive secretary, Girl Scouts
Executive secretary, Boy Scouts
Superintendent of the private school for boys
Director of public health nursing (a new member)
Director of a home for children (a new member)
Case worker of the State Public Aid Commission
(a new member)

The relationship of the Professional Committee to the
project staff is on a group basis. The project staff shares
its problems and plans with the Professional Committee during the scheduled meetings. The problems and plans are presented by a member of the project staff to the committee.
Advantages and disadvantages of various proposals and patterns of action are considered, and suggestions are made.
Usually a consensus is reached, and a workable plan is evolved.
The opinions and proposals are not considered as final answers to questions, since the Professional Committee consid-

ers its deliberations advisory rather than binding on the
project staff. The meetings are quite informal and are mutually helpful to members of both groups.

The first duty of the Professional Committee was to
select people to participate in the training seminar. The
people were selected to provide a variety of interests and
occupational skills, along with an aptitude for work with
children. Few persons were admitted to the training seminar primarily upon their own request. A high per cent of
those selected took and completed the seminar. After the
counselor teams were formed, the Professional Committee followed their progress closely and gave careful thought to the
problems confronting the teams.

During the past year the Professional Committee has devoted much consideration to the progress of the project. It
was kept very well informed about the proposed plans of the
project staff. The committee considered such problems as
what information should be available to parents and how the
information might be most effectively given to parents. The
problem of an effective working relationship of the project
team with the child was explored very carefully. As the
problem resolved itself, the committee was vitally concerned
with each progressive step. The problem of keeping the Professional Committee alert to the evolving program was ever
present. This was done through regular progress reports.
An excellent relationship between the staff and the Professional Committee has supplied a supportive approach which
has been mutually helpful.

Another project during the year was the preparation
and publishing of a directory of the community resources.
The need for such a directory had long been felt by the
agencies of the local community. The Professional Committee
worked with the consultant staff and with members of the sem
inar in this effort. It is expected that the teams and loca
agencies will be greatly aided by knowing the community resources available for reference and referral.

Several points requiring consideration by the Professional Committee are now forging into the foreground. The
problem of full integration of community resources, especially as represented by the Professional Committee, must
be resolved. The full impact of the community's resources
must be brought to bear upon a co-ordinated plan to help

each child with his developmental problems. The committee
also must think through its relationship with the project
staff, and how the work can best be planned so that each
child in the community can derive the most from growing up
in this city. The essential question is: How can we best
merge our thoughts, our plans, and our agency action into a
single bold effort to help our boys and girls?

The Schools and the Project

Basically the Youth Development Program is a community
program and not a school program. Essentially, it is a co-
operative program of all the agencies of the community that
serve youth. The public school is one of the community
agencies through which the Commission works. Pupils from
certain grades of the school are being studied through the
co-operation of the instructional staff of the school, the
Commission staff, and members of other co-operating organizations or agencies.

Before beginning this project, the Commission explained
the nature of the program, its objectives, and the organizational plan to the instructional staff of the school, the
administrators, and the Board of Education. The approval of
the Board of Education was secured.

A member of the administrative staff of the school was
named liaison officer to promote co-operation between the
school and the Commission. This staff member spent one summer at the University of Chicago in training for his duties.
He is the official representative of the school before the
Commission and the person who keeps the school informed concerning the work of the Commission.

In preparation for the work of the Community Youth Development Program, more than thirty members of the teaching
staff of the public school were enrolled in training cours-
es. Members of the Commission staff instructed these teachers in the methods and techniques to be used in the study of
boys and girls in this project.

The first year was devoted to training adult leaders of
the community, screening the children of the fourth grade,
and organizing information obtained through a variety of
tests given to pupils of the fourth and sixth grades. Teachers assisted the Commission staff members in this work. The
facilities of the schools were used wherever needed, and

necessary data concerning pupils were provided from school records or by the teaching staff.

A co-operative testing program is being designed to meet the needs of both the school and the project. Experimentation with a variety of tests is under way in an attempt to find the most practical, effective, and efficient testing program.

The Commission is interested in aiding a community to find the best methods of discovering very early the children with special problems and special abilities. The school is interested in designing a school program that will more nearly meet the needs of children with special problems and special abilities. A close co-operative relationship is mutually beneficial.

A realization of the objectives of the Community Youth Commission should provide a community approach to its youth problem that will be most helpful to the schools. The public schools expect to receive aid in planning a school program that will more nearly meet the needs of all youth.

The desire of the school officials and of the Commission is that this co-operative undertaking may prove to be a source of information for other school systems interested in improving the offerings of their schools to these two general groups of children--the gifted group and the maladjusted group.

Appendix A(1)

PARENT REPORT FORM - PROFILE OF A CHILD WITH HIGH SCORES

Percentile Scores

95%   50%

1. INTELLECTUAL APTITUDE for doing general school work and similar tasks. . . . . .

2. PROBLEM SOLVING APTITUDE for using common sense in figuring out practical problems.

3. COMPREHENSION APTITUDE for noticing details of things and understanding their meaning. . . . .

4. ANALYTIC APTITUDE for identifying specific patterns in a complex design. . . . . .

5. VERBAL APTITUDE for expressing himself in words and understanding words. . . . . .

6. SPATIAL APTITUDE for imagining different views of objects by looking at their drawings. . . . .

7. REASONING APTITUDE for figuring out the reason behind things. . . . .

8. DRAWING APTITUDE for expressing himself in painting and drawing. . . . .

9. MUSIC APTITUDE for expressing himself in some form of music. . . . .

10. SOCIAL COOPERATION, the ability to work and play with others harmoniously:
    with adults . . . .
    with children . . . .

11. SOCIAL CONFIDENCE, the ability to feel at ease and enjoy oneself with other people:
    with adults . . . .
    with children . . . .

12. SOCIAL LEADERSHIP, the ability to make it possible for people to work or play together effectively
    as seen by adults . . . .
    as seen by children . . . .

13. SOCIAL ACCEPTABILITY, being liked and wanted as a friend by other children. . . . . .

Appendix A(2)

PARENT REPORT FORM - PROFILE OF A CHILD WITH LOW SCORES

Percentile Scores

50%

1. INTELLECTUAL APTITUDE for doing general school work and similar tasks. . . .

2. PROBLEM SOLVING APTITUDE for using common sense in figuring out practical problems. . .

3. COMPREHENSION APTITUDE for noticing details of things and understanding their meaning. . . . .

4. ANALYTIC APTITUDE for identifying specific patterns in a complex design. . . . .

5. VERBAL APTITUDE for expressing himself in words and understanding words. . . . .

6. SPATIAL APTITUDE for imagining different views of objects by looking at their drawings. . . . .

7. REASONING APTITUDE for figuring out the reason behind things. . . . . . .

8. DRAWING APTITUDE for expressing himself in painting and drawing. . . . . . .

9. MUSIC APTITUDE for expressing himself in some form of music. . . . .

10. SOCIAL COOPERATION, the ability to work and play with others harmoniously:
with adults. . . . .
with children. . . . .

11. SOCIAL CONFIDENCE, the ability to feel at ease and enjoy oneself with other people:
with adults. . . . .
with children. . . . .

12. SOCIAL LEADERSHIP, the ability to make it possible for people to work or play together effectively
as seen by adults. . . . . . .
as seen by children. . . . . .

13. SOCIAL ACCEPTABILITY, being liked and wanted as a friend by other children. . . .

INTERPRETATION OF PARENT REPORT
FORM, AUTUMN, 1952

1. <u>Intellectual Aptitude</u> (<u>SRA Primary Mental Abili-</u>
<u>ties, ages 8-10</u>): This is an I.Q. score which shows to
what degree a child has the kinds of intelligence useful
in achieving academic success. This score might be useful
in deciding whether or not a child should attempt college
or other higher-education work. The score is a combination
of scores for the following areas: memory, verbal meaning,
word fluency, space, number, perception, and reasoning.
This test has been regularly administered by the schools to
children in the fourth grade.

2. <u>Problem-Solving Aptitude</u> (<u>Davis-Eells Games: Cul-</u>
<u>ture Fair Intelligence Test</u>): This is an I.Q. score which
indicates the kind of intelligence useful in everyday living. The effect of a child's experience, his ability to
use words, and his negative attitudes toward school and
tests (if he has them) are reduced to a minimum.

3. <u>Comprehension Aptitude</u> (<u>Draw-a-Man</u>): This is an
I.Q. score which indicates the kind of intelligence necessary in forming ideas and concepts out of our experience
and observation, understanding various aspects of what we
experience, and pointing these things out to ourselves.

4. <u>Analytic Aptitude</u> (<u>Concealed Figures Test</u>): This
involves the specific ability to "make sense" of an otherwise confusing situation by seeing in it things with which
we are already familiar. This ability would be helpful in
work which requires creative effort and in the solution of
complex problems.

5. <u>Verbal Aptitude</u> (<u>PMA 11-17 V</u>): This ability is
important in the many vocational and interest fields where
success depends on how well a person can use words, such as
secretarial work, selling, writing, teaching. It is also
very important in academic success in high school and especially in college.

6. <u>Spatial Aptitude</u> (<u>PMA 11-17 S</u>): This ability is
important in any field where one must be able to think clearly about how things look or work in space. Important in
such fields as drafting, designing, art, surgery, mechanics,
engineering, and architecture.

7. Reasoning Aptitude (PMA 11-17 R): This involves
the ability to think abstractly and to figure out the relationship between things. Important in higher academic and
professional work.

10. Social Co-operation (Behavior Description Chart and
Who Are They?): This shows how a child acts with other people. A high score shows that he works or plays well with
them; a low score shows that he does things which conflict
with the activity and desires of the group he is with. The
first score is based on the observation of the teacher who
is a part of the child's group, the second on the observation of the other children in the group.

11. Social Confidence (Behavior Description Chart and
Who Are They?): This shows how a child feels within himself
about his relations with other people, in terms of being
able to express his own feelings and desires and to behave
in ways which make him happy with them. A high score would
mean that he acts pretty much the way he feels, and this
feeling is likely to be confident and happy; a low score
would mean that he is more withdrawn and hesitant to express
himself. The first score is based on the observation of the
teacher, and the second on the observation of the children.

12. Social Leadership (Behavior Description Chart and
Who Are They?): This score represents the capacity of a
child for initiating and carrying responsibility for activities. The first score is of leadership as seen by the teacher and other adults, and the second as seen by the children.

13. Social Acceptability (Who Are They?): This is a
score on the qualities for friendship as rated only by the
children. A high score indicates he is chosen as a friend
by many children, a low score by few children.

APPENDIX C

EXPLANATORY LETTER TO PARENTS

November, 1952

To the Parents of Fifth-Graders at ------- School:

This meeting is called for the purpose of reporting to you the results of tests that were given to all fourth-graders in the city last year. It is aimed to help you find out what things your child can do best and what things he is less good at, so that you can better know how to plan for your child's best development.

Before dealing with the test results of your child, you might appreciate some general information about the Youth Development Commission that parents frequently ask about. One question is: "What is the Commission and why is it interested in knowing about and helping my child?" The Commission is composed of a large number of people from the city who are working in this project in the interests of boys and girls. The Commission is working closely with the schools and many youth-serving agencies in the city. The purpose of the Commission is to help parents find whatever sort of aid they need and want in guiding the growth of their children.

Another question frequently asked is: "Why was only the fourth grade tested last year?" First of all, we had to choose one grade because it was too big a job for us to work with any more children. The fourth grade was chosen because fourth-graders are old enough to be able to take the tests and young enough that plans can be made for them with a good chance of being successfully carried out. There are perhaps other questions in your mind about this project, and we will be glad to answer them as best we can this evening.

We are ready to report to you what has been discovered about your child--his strong points and weak points. Our tests on which the ratings were made are quite accurate, but of course are not infallible. As your child grows older, there will likely be some changes in his performance, and a few further tests will be given from time to time.

The individual results for your own child will be given you tonight by a counselor in a private interview. It is important that your own knowledge of the child at home be

added to the ratings from the tests to give the best all-
round picture of his capabilities. From these two sources
you and the counselor might be able to discuss questions
you have about your child, your concerns for him, and how
you can help him make the most of his future.

    We expect that many of you will want to discuss these
things more at length than we will have time for tonight.
We will be happy to talk with you whenever you like, and
you can make further arrangements with your counselor tonight, or by calling on the Commission office any time.

                         Sincerely yours,

                         YOUTH DEVELOPMENT COMMISSI

APPENDIX D

CRITERIA FOR RATING CHILDREN'S DRAWINGS

In judging the merits of the drawings of the children, we will need to decide what characteristics of the pictures we think are important to judge and then find a way to give scores to the pictures according to their merit in these. It has been suggested that any art product has physical, mental, and spiritual qualities. The Art Committee might look for and judge the following things in the drawings: (1) the ability of the child to represent an object (physical qualities), (2) the technical ability of the child (physical qualities), (3) aesthetic qualities of the picture (mental qualities), and (4) the originality or creativity of the artist (spiritual qualities). These characteristics are not completely inseparable. There is some overlap in them.

Representational ability.--This is almost completely a developmental characteristic; that is, as children grow older they pass through one stage after another in their ability to represent an object on paper. This ability indicates their maturity in art development, and is one way of judging their artistic talent, since talented children are usually more advanced in this respect than average children.

Technical ability.--This is the ability of the child to control the medium he is using. This is partly a developmental characteristic, since, as children grow older, they become stronger and more co-ordinated. It is also partly a measure of training. It is also a measure of ability in that, presumably, some children's mind-muscle control is and always will be better than that of other children and they therefore can control the medium much better than the other children can.

Aesthetic qualities.--These are the rare, less tangible qualities that contribute the most toward making a picture beautiful. They show the mental, conceptual grasp the artist has on his subject. Such qualities are not primarily developmental but show up at all ages. These rare qualities are not absolutely different from those found in average drawings but represent a more intense manifestation of an otherwise frequently observed characteristic.

121

Originality.--By originality is meant the creativeness
that the artist displays in his work. He may be creative
by communicating something about himself or by producing a
novel drawing. He may put his own experience or feeling
into the picture in such a way that every person who sees
the picture can apply it to his own experience or feeling,
or he may use the medium to produce results which are different.

Representational Ability

Instructions: Decide on the number on the continuum which this drawing rates. A high score means that the child can represent the object well according to the criteria below. A low score means that he cannot. Enter the score in this score sheet.

Continuum <u>1</u>   2   3   4   <u>5</u>

1. Primitive schema

Schematic symbols are used to represent the object. The symbols are drawn in an incomplete manner. Parts of the object are omitted; for example, the whole body of a human figure may be missing, thus representing it by head and legs only. Various parts are represented with fewer details and less definite contour than in the schematic stage.

2. Schema

People, animals, and other objects are represented with the help of simplified symbols which reduce the shape of the object to a combination of ovals, rounds, squares, and dots. The child outlines the different parts of the objects separately and unites them by adding one part to the next. Different views of the object will be combined into one drawing, or different objects into one composition, but as if seen from various points of view. Objects which are hidden from sight are nevertheless represented.

3. Mixed

Some objects drawn schematically, some drawn true to appearance, or objects which are in part schematic and in part true to appearance.

4. True to appearance

The attempt is made to represent objects as they appear, i.e., in outlines, proportions, colors, dimensions which are similar to their appearance. No third dimension is attempted; therefore flatness of drawing is present. A single point of vantage or observation is maintained; several objects in a picture are assembled in such a way that hidden objects or part of them which cannot be seen simultaneously remain also hidden in the drawing.

5. Perspective

This is an extension of the true-to-appearance stage insofar as objects are represented as true in appearance with the addition of a more or less correct linear perspective and representation of distance. This stage also includes a sitting figure or a three-quarter view of a figure.

Technical Ability

Instructions: Decide on the number of the continuum which this drawing rates in each of the areas listed below. Not all the areas can be used on all the assignments. In some cases, the drawings are mixed, for example, some areas

being ragged and scratchy and others bold and saturated. It
should be decided what is predominant in the picture, and
the picture judged on that. Enter score into record sheet.

Line technique

1. Used hesitating, timid, ragged line. The artist
   seemed not to know what to draw or was unsure of
   himself in drawing it. Scratchy.
2. Clumsy and/or heavy line.
3. Decisive, firm line. The artist seemed to know
   what he wanted to draw.
4. Bold.
5. Discriminating, subtle, and/or bold line. The
   artist knows what he wanted to draw and how to do
   it. He may even show intentional lack of clarity
   or appropriate indefiniteness in outline.

Continuum   1   2   3   4   5

Area technique

1. Ragged, scratchy area.
2. Smooth area; the area fully and uniformly covered,
   flat.
3. Bold area; saturated, vigorous use of color.
4. Graded areas; step-wise gradation between areas
   and/or blended area.
5. Textured, or molded areas.

Continuum   1   2   3   4   5

Flexibility of objects

1. Objects stiff, wooden; inappropriately cramped. No
   freedom in number, kind, or means of depicting them.
   Some objects don't seem to fit the picture, others
   do.

3. Some objects stiff, others flexible. Not much freedom in the number, kinds, or means of depicting them

5. Objects fit; are flexible, graceful, symmetrical or
   forceful, depending on their nature. Freedom in the
   objects. Lifelike.

Continuum   1   2   3   4   5

Aesthetic Qualities

Instructions: Decide on the number on the continuum
which this drawing rates in each of the areas listed below.
Not all the areas can be used on all the assignments. Enter
the score in the score sheet.

Compositional unity

1. Organization not attempted, random organization.
   No concept present of position in space; related
   only functionally, for example, a person is near
   another person only because he is handing him something.
2. Linear organization through a ground line or stand
   line on which all the objects are placed. May have
   more than one ground line.

3. Objects related to each other in space, not merely functionally, and a certain amount of unity achieved through this relation. Drawings may be highly organized in a formal, decorative pattern.

4-5. Only one object presented, but well proportioned, symmetrical, well placed within the space, rhythmic lines emphasizing the object.

4-5. Successful, unusual organization obtained: through proper emphasis, obtained by subordinating marginal objects to the central object; through balance, obtained through spacing and relative position of the objects; by selectivity of objects to present a central theme.

Continuum 1   2   3   4   5

Color

1. Indiscriminate, unrealistic use of color, random selection of colors, colors not related to each other indicating no attempt to take account of one color when using another, bright colors producing a displeasing effect or timid, weak. Unpleasing pattern or lack of pattern.

3. Good color sense and value. Harmony in use of colors; over-all effect considered, colors used in relation to each other, but no outstanding effect obtained. Bright, clear colors used with no blending or unusual contrasts.

5. Outstanding contrasts or other effects obtained through blending, spotting; emphasis gained by effective subordination of less important colors. Discriminating use of color. Superior. Pleasing pattern; outstanding color sense and value.

Continuum 1   2   3   4   5

Artistic movement--path of vision

1. No path of vision for the eye to follow; picture broken up; sectioned.

3. Path of vision more or less present; may be broken or only partly successful; some major portions of the picture are left out of the path; eye may leave the picture.

5. Path of vision successful; eye stays in the picture; major parts of the picture included in the path.

Continuum 1   2   3   4   5

Originality

Instructions: Decide on the number on the continuum which this drawing rates in each of the areas listed below. Both areas should be used in scoring all the drawing assignments. Enter the score in the score sheet.

Creative liberty

1. This child was bizarre in his drawing; went so far beyond convention and the assignment that he seemed to lack either understanding of the assignment or control of his impulses. Rejected the assignment, copied or traced another drawing.

3. This person was mechanically bound by the assignment, showed no experimentativeness or inventiveness in any parts of the drawing. Did not produce more than a conventional or stereotyped drawing. Handled the assignment routinely. Was not stimulated to rise above mediocrity.

5. This person took liberties with the assignment; deviated enough from the assignment in order to represent his own experiences or preferences. Took the opportunity as a means of self-expression. Was inventive and got outside the usual conventions in depicting his work.

Continuum   1   2   3   4   5

Communicativeness

1. This picture is dull in all its aspects. Communicates nothing fresh and vital about the artist's experience or feeling.

3. This picture is predominantly dull, but is vital in some of its aspects. Leaves one questioning and uncertain.

5. This person gives a freshness and eagerness to his drawing, communicates an experience, conveys a feeling. This person has insight into his subject and can communicate it.

APPENDIX E

CALENDAR OF THE TRAINING PROGRAM

Lecture Topic or Presentation	Subgroup Meetings

SEPTEMBER, 1951

Introduction to the Project--Staff	No subgroup meeting
Developmental Tasks--Staff	Case 1. Normal, active boy. Three subgroups were formed; an instructor led each.

OCTOBER, 1951

The Peer Society--Staff	Case 2. Lawrence, normal, boy
The Aggressively Maladjusted Child--Staff	Case 3. Jed, aggressive, maladjusted boy
The Gifted Child--Staff and Member of Professional Committee	Case 3. Continued
The Withdrawn Child--Staff	Case 3. Concluded
The Family--Professor of Education in the Local College	Case 4. Elsie, withdrawn girl

NOVEMBER, 1951

Socioeconomic Differences in Child Development--Staff	Case 4. Concluded
An Experimental Approach to Preschool Training--Professor Samuel Kirk, University of Illinois	Panel discussion of treatment procedures, participated in by staff, counselors, and member of Professional Committe
A "Team" demonstration of treatment procedures--Staff and Member of Professional Committee	Movie: The Feeling of Rejection. Discussion led by staff member
Personality Development: Demonstration of counseling session--Staff	Case 5. Roberta, gifted girl

DECEMBER, 1951

Physical Development--Staff	Case 5. Continued
The Mental-Hygiene Movement-- Miss Helen Natwick, Consultant Nurse, Bureau of Maternal and Child Health, State Department of Public Health	Case 5. Concluded

Sociodrama of group problems: No subgroup meeting
  "Good Team" and "Bad Team"--
  Staff and Counselors

JANUARY, 1952

Development of Moral Character   Case 6. Ernest, play ther-
  --Staff   apy
Movie: <u>The Terrible Two's and</u>   Case 6. Continued
  <u>the Trusting Three's</u>
Group Leadership--Staff   Case 6. Concluded
Play Therapy--Dr. Paul Bowman   Case 7. Tom, play therapy
  (at that time of University
  of Louisville)
(First-semester examination for those taking the course for
  credit)
Review of Preadolescent Period-- Case 8. Jerry, play therapy
  Staff

FEBRUARY, 1952

Structure of Personality and   Case 9. The ----- family.
  Its Development in the Family   Home life of the mother
  --Staff   and father
Parent-Child Relationships--   Case 9. Continued. Two
  Executive Director of Family   sons
  Service Agency
Sibling Relationships--Staff   Case 9. Continued. Two
                                        daughters

Illustrated Lecture on Team   Counselors decide on roles,
  Roles--Staff   make sociometric choices

MARCH, 1952

Report on results of member   Case 10. Marian West,
  role choice, sociometric   Family Service case
  tests. Discussion--Staff
Screening Devices, Intellectual   Case 10. Concluded
  Aptitude Tests--Staff
Screening Devices for Personal-   Introduction of local
  ity Maladjustment--Staff   case. Formation of
                                        balanced subgroups
Professional Treatment of Con-   Local case, continued
  fidential Data--Staff

APRIL, 1952

Analysis of Community Resources --Staff	Local case, continued
Movie: <u>Angry Boy</u>	No subgroup meeting
Analysis of Community Resources, continued--Staff	Local case, continued. Set up interviews to get data on community resources

(Formation of nine balanced teams for the three subgroups.
Each team selected a local case to study, including the
local cases begun in the subgroups.)

Importance of Teams in the Project--Staff	Team cases, continued

MAY, 1952

Team cases, continued	Team cases, continued
Team cases, continued	"Trouble-shooting" ses- sion--Staff

Training seminar party
(Final examination for those taking the course for credit)

Each team met once during the last two weeks in May
and made a diagnostic summary of the case on which they were
working and set up plans for summer meetings. Each team was
urged to take another case for the summer months. Five
teams did, and four teams did not.

APPENDIX F$_{(1)}$
LIST OF TRAINING ACTIVITIES, 1951-52

A. Lecture periods
B. Presentation of principles and concepts dealing with the physical, personal, and social growth of children
C. Presentation of concepts dealing with therapy
D. Presentation of concepts dealing with group dynamics
E. Presentation of plans and procedures to be used on the project
F. Subgroup meetings following lecture periods
G. Team meetings
H. Case studies of therapy
I. Case studies of the types of maladjusted children to be dealt with on this project
J. Demonstrations
K. Movies
L. Discussions of aspects of the course with others, no instructor being present
M. "Extra-curricular" groups, e.g., therapy and group dynamics meetings
N. Reading in connection with the training course
O. Making community contacts, e.g., interviewing, getting information, etc.
P. Taking examinations
Q. Studying and reviewing course content
R. Filling in evaluation forms and questionnaires
S. Consultation or informal discussion outside the classroom with instructors
T. Study of actual cases from the community

EVALUATION FORM

Listed below are a number of statements describing the activities which made up the training program. On the attached sheet is a list of the activities of the training program. Which of these activities would you describe with the descriptive statements? Put the letters of the activities in front of as many of the descriptive statements as you think they most readily belong with.

1. These activities (name at least three) were satisfying, outstanding, and stimulating to me; I enjoyed them the most.

2. These activities (name at least three) left little impression on me; I had almost forgotten about them.

3. These activities (name at least two) were frustrating and disappointing to me; I enjoyed them the least.

4. These activities (name at least three) were instructive; they enabled me to increase my understanding and helped me think more clearly; I learned the most from them.

5. These activities (name at least three) were less instructive; I learned little from them; they presented material which I felt I already knew.

6. These activities (name at least two) confused me, left me up in the air, did not seem to make sense.

7. These activities (name at least three) were strong points in the program, and should be repeated in a future training course.

8. These activities (name at least three) were only moderately successful, need to be timed better, need to be improved for a future course.

9. These activities (name at least three) would need extensive modification in a future course.

10. I did not attend or take part in these activities.

Add any additional comments you wish to make below. (We are especially interested in your recommendations to 8 and 9.)

Do not sign your name, but please indicate by a check if you are a school teacher _____
            not a school teacher _____

BEHAVIOR DESCRIPTION CHART

Directions: In each of the sets of descriptive statements below, pick out two statements. (1) Pick out that
statement which you find fits the child most aptly--the one
which the child is most like. (2) Then pick out the statement which the child is least like. Place the letters of
these statements on the record sheet under the number corresponding to the set of statements. Do not be concerned
if the statement does not apply exactly, and do not dwell
too long upon your decision. Go through the entire chart
for one child at a time. Experience shows that the ratings
can be completed in just a few minutes per child.

---

1. A. Others come to him for help
   B. Causes disturbances
   C. Is easily irritated, flustered, or upset
   D. Reports those who break the rules
   E. Shows emotions in a restrained way

2. A. Resentful
   B. Is unsure of himself
   C. Other children are eager to be near him or on
      his side
   D. Criticizes other people
   E. Interested in other people's opinions and ac-
      tivities

3. A. Avoids competition
   B. Shows off, attention-getter
   C. Is self-confident
   D. Enjoys being a part of the group without taking
      the lead
   E. Usually willing to share with others

4. A. Is extremely quiet and passive
   B. Is popular with all his classmates
   C. Is boastful
   D. Is friendly only when others make advances
   E. Likes to daydream, but can bring himself back
      to reality when there is work to be done

5. A. Frequently gets into fights
   B. Helps to make and enforce rules
   C. Seems anxious and fearful
   D. In group work often insists that his way is better
   E. Is generous when in the mood

6. A. Makes sensible, practical plans
   B. Breaks rules
   C. Needs much prodding
   D. Dislikes criticism
   E. Accepts responsibility when it is assigned to him

7. A. Avoids attention
   B. Pitches in and helps when things need to be done
   C. Claims he is not treated fairly by others
   D. Does not care what others think
   E. Does not stand out from the crowd

8. A. Takes an active part in group projects and other
      activities
   B. Appears to have little concern or interest in
      what goes on around him
   C. Others cannot work with him
   D. Polite
   E. Assertive

9. A. Rarely asked for his opinion by others
   B. Defiant toward authority and disobedient
   C. Figures out things for himself
   D. Avoids trouble, if possible
   E. Sometimes disturbs others by laughing or talking,
      but stops at once when reminded

10. A. Sensitive, touchy, hurt by criticism
    B. Lies to get out of trouble
    C. Is a natural leader
    D. Finds excuses when his work is not done
    E. Usually willing to share with others

11. A. Cheats in games
    B. Is tense or ill at ease when reciting or appear-
       ing before a group
    C. Works for the welfare of his class, team, club,
       or school
    D. About as honest as the average
    E. Enjoys a conversation

12. A. Quarrelsome
    B. Likes jobs which give him responsibility
    C. Avoids games
    D. Does his share, but does not seek leadership
    E. Friendly to a limited group

13. A. So colorless that group would not miss his presence
    B. Creates a sense of reassurance in others: gives
       them confidence in themselves
    C. Is impulsive and easily excited
    D. Is a good follower
    E. Is usually courteous to other children

14. A. Plans ahead
    B. Becomes discouraged easily
    C. Steals small amounts of money and other property
    D. Finishes work promptly, but in careless fashion
    E. Is about as honest as most persons his age

15. A. Is bossy in relations with other children
    B. Is quick to see valuable things in other people's
       suggestions
    C. Is hard to know
    D. Gets along in social groups about as well as the
       average person
    E. Pleasant to talk with but seldom initiates a con-
       versation

16. A. Is easily confused
    B. Can be depended on by an adult leader of a group
       to do his share
    C. Is always thinking up alibis
    D. Carries through an undertaking about as well as
       others his age
    E. Is often pulled away from the main job by side
       interests

17. A. Contributes new ideas to a group project
    B. Lacks confidence in himself
    C. Plays mean tricks on others
    D. Gives advice only when asked
    E. Will make some sacrifices for others

18. A. Appears unhappy, unable to enjoy himself
    B. Is alert and well-poised
    C. Is rude and unfriendly
    D. Is quiet and seems content with himself
    E. Is boisterous

WHO ARE THEY?

March 1952

    Here are some descriptions of different kinds of boys and girls. Read each description and ask yourself: "Which boys and girls in our group are like this?" Look over the list of names of your group, to find the ones that fit each description. Put the letter of the description <u>in front of</u> as many names of boys and girls as you think it readily belongs with.

    Do not sign your name to this paper. Do not put any letters next to your own name.

A. Who are the boys and girls that make good plans?
    Put an <u>A</u> in front of the name of every boy and girl who is like this.

B. Who are the good leaders? They are leaders in several things.
    Put a <u>B</u> in front of the name of every boy and girl who is like this.

C. Who are the boys and girls that stay out of games. They don't like to play hard.
    Put a <u>C</u> in front of the name of every boy and girl who is like this.

D. Who are the ones that break rules; rules of the school and rules of games?

E. Who are the ones that seem to understand things most easily, out of school and in school?

F. Who are the boys and girls that always work for the good of their class, or their team, or their playmates?

G. Who are the boys and girls that lie and steal a little bit?

H. Who are the ones that are too shy to make friends easily? It is hard to get to know them.

I. Who are the ones that complain about things? Nothing satisfies them. They want to have their own way.

J. Who are the boys and girls that are very smart at games and other things? They have a lot of good ideas.

K. Who are the ones that get bothered and upset when they are called on to talk or recite? They cannot tell as much as they really know.

L. Who are the most popular boys and girls?

M. Who are the boys and girls that you do not notice? You just don't think about whether they are present or not.

N. Who are the ones that are timid and afraid to take chance

O. Which boys and girls quarrel and get mad easily?

P. Who are the ones that are sure to have ideas for games an other interesting things to do, both out of school and in school?

Q. Who are the ones that are mean and cruel to other children?

R. Who are the boys and girls you would like for your best friends?
   Put an R in front of the name of every one you would like for your best friend.

S. Who are the ones you would not like for your friends?
   Put an S in front of the name of every one you would not like for a friend.